Welcon

MW00933947

Since you picked up this book, perhaps you were attracted by its title. But my guess is you are an "animal lover." Until the day I started as Dr. Weaver's dolphin research boat captain, I was not of the "animal loving" mindset. Almost immediately I was drawn to the obvious intelligence and complex cultural interactions of these mammals as they negotiated the local waters and their encounters with each other.

You are about to embark on a rare journey, courtesy of Dr. Weaver's enlightening observations and insights into the social world of one community of Florida bottlenose dolphins.

Over recorded time, mankind has found dolphins to be a source of fascination, adoration, and inspiration. The scientific community interested in dolphins has for the most part focused on dolphin population sizes and locations. I see this as a justifiable but narrow perspective.

In contrast, not only has Dr. Weaver endeavored over the past 13 years to chronicle this important but hard-to-obtain information. She is the first person I am aware of to focus her study on a three-dimensional perspective: long-term, year-round study of dolphin social behavior without seasonal, personnel, or funding interruptions. Her observations provide unique views of how individuals and groups of local dolphins move through their likes, dislikes, frustrations, survival techniques, sexual encounters, and social development.

As for me, after 1000 dolphin surveys with her to date and over 8000 hours on the water, I can honestly admit that I have crossed over and now find each trip a fascinating never-ending story - perhaps even a learning mechanism for our society. Dolphins have been in place as we know them for over 5 million years and continue to demonstrate a perception of forward thinking and tolerance of each other that we as humans should aspire to.

So sit back, relax, and float along on Dr. Weaver's "Enchanted River." I'm sure these vignettes will give you intriguing insights into a species that we should perhaps emulate. I hope they calm your mind and help erase our never-ending human neurosis.

Captain John Heidemann

Secrets behind the Dolphin Smile

25 Amazing Things Dolphins Do

Ann Weaver, Ph.D.

JAASAS ACADEMIC PRESS
JA
DIVERSIFIED EXPLORATION AND EDUCATION SERVICES

For more information or permission to use material from this book, contact at annstats54@gmail.com.

Weaver, Ann. (2017). Secrets behind the Dolphin Smile – 25 Amazing Things Dolphins Do. Jaasas Academic Press: Treasure Island, FL. 146 pp. ISBN-10: 1973500361. ISBN-13: 978-1973500360.

Dedicated to Animal Lovers the World Over

Animals are "different teachers." May we strive to understand their different ways of existing, as well as respect and learn from our interactions.

Table of Contents

Rules of Conduct

1. One Helluva Snuggie (Welcome to my World)
2. Saga Dances with the Devil
3. Burning Bonds of Love
4. Dolphin Sense of Fair Play
5. Clara the Kidnapper and Simon the Savior
6. A Dolphin First Responder

Seaside Showmanship

7. Dying for Attention
8. Sylvia's High Flying Romance
9. Shall We Dance?
10. Legendary Lust or Fair is Fair?
11. Sometimes You Need a Bigger Hammer
12. Dressing Up for a Dark Party
13. The Princess and the Pea

Behavior toward the Boat

14. Our Favorite Flirt
15. Mystery at McDonald's
16. The Accidental Easter Bonnet
17. How a Dolphin Might Launch a Conversation
18. The Dolphins and Dr. Dolittle
19. Seaside Bait-and-Switch
20. Spooky Action at a Distance

A Teaser of Bull Behavior

21. As a Matter of Fact, I Will Share
22. Afterglow
23. Pick on Someone Your Own Size!
24. Scraped Knees or Sharpening Swords?

Category of its Own

25. Who Is Innocent among Us?

*** Rules of Conduct ***

1. One Helluva Snuggie

PHOTO BY ANN WEAVER, Ph.D., NOAA 1088-1815, 7/23/2006

They Watch Us Watching Them

***

People who go behind-the-scenes in the ape house at the zoo are instructed to stand back from the cages of the chimps, gorillas, and orangutans they meet. Ape arms are longer and stronger than human arms, and captive apes look for amusing activities to break their routine. In any chance (or intentional!) encounter between an ape and a person, the ape will prevail.

A highly experienced ape keeper at the Phoenix Zoo knew all this, of course. Moreover, he was on excellent terms with the apes in his charge, including a huge male orangutan. The day came when the keeper moved closer to the ape's cage than usual and gave the alert orange ape an interesting opportunity to change his routine. The ape was in his bedroom cage watching his keeper sweep hay into a pile. The keeper turned his back to the ape for a moment and bent forward. This let the rim of his underwear peek out of the top of his jeans. Quick as a flash, the orangutan grabbed the rim of the underwear and yanked it. This is what, in the Midwest of America, we call a "snuggie."

But the orangutan was so strong that he yanked the keeper's underwear completely out of his jeans!

That is what anyone would call one helluva snuggie!

As if that keeper's snuggie was not memorable enough, the orangutan rushed out into his public display enclosure with his prize, where he sat like a king on a throne wearing the white underwear on his orange hair like a crown - for the next two hours, which is how long it took the keeper to persuade the ape to trade the underwear for something more interesting!

***

The orangutan was expressing himself, theatrically and memorably, to be sure, as have all of the apes I have known or studied before studying dolphins. The orangutan underwear story felt like a good way to introduce bottlenose dolphins who have also expressed themselves theatrically and memorably – though not on par with stealing a man's underwear while he is wearing it and then wearing it themselves!

These stories of self-expression at sea whisper volumes about the bottlenose dolphins' intellectual, emotional, and social abilities – especially because these are stories about what *wild* dolphins at sea do naturally. They are not beholden to us or our boat in any way; certainly not the way captive animals are beholden to their keepers. The 25 amazing things dolphins do along the "Enchanted River" reveal a complex society organized to face challenges that, in many ways, parallel the challenges we face in human society: the individual doing all he or she can to survive, find companionship and others to rely on, protect the young, avoid danger, and play by the rules or suffer the consequences.

*****

Welcome to my World of the "Enchanted River"

The "Enchanted River" is my dolphin project's study area. I am an animal behaviorist who is fascinated by how animals do what nature designed them to do, the science of ethology; I am an ethologist. I have been fortunate to have worked with or studied over 200 animal species so far[i] and even more fortunate to have studied bottlenose dolphins living free in five different seas around the world. For the last 13 years, I have intensively studied the free-ranging bottlenose dolphins who live in the tranquil venue of my western Florida study site, the "Enchanted River," where they generously allow us to watch their lives. This book is about them.

They have given us countless moments of unforgettable self-expression, 25 of which I share here. Some episodes are unique to the individual dolphin whose story is told. Others are examples of self-expression that several dolphins have been seen doing.

The stories can be read in any order but are presented in five sets. The first set, *Rules of Conduct*, show how dolphins treat each other. The second set, *Seaside Showmanship,* are stories of dolphins showing off or *stylin'* for each other. The third set, *Behavior towards the Boat,* gives a glimpse of what the dolphins might think about our boat, or us. The fourth set, *A Teaser of Bull Behavior*, lets us glance into the complex political worlds of adult bottlenose dolphin males, whom I call bulls. The final story set, *Category of Its Own*, is the most humbling gift they have given us.

Initially, the goal of my study was to document any changes in local free-ranging bottlenose dolphins during a 5-year bridge construction project over The Pass between the Intracoastal Waterway and Gulf of Mexico. I work under federal permit* to identify best practices for conservation. We documented a significant decline in dolphin numbers and have continued monitoring to see if their numbers increased back up to baseline (happily, they have!).

The "Enchanted River" is a winding stretch of Intracoastal Waterway (6 miles/9.6 km long and 0.5-1 mile/0.8-1.6 km wide), flanked by a combination of waterfront houses and unaltered natural coastline. We survey it 2-3 times a week in a 20' (6 m) motor boat that we call "*Miss Behavin'*."

The dolphins are untrained and live free at sea. We have identified 370 dolphins to date by natural markings on their dorsal fins, the fin on their backs that is visible when they surface to breathe. We watch them like TV except that I study their behavior closely and document everything while US Coast Guard Captain John Heidemann pilots our course. We do not feed, pet, or play with them. Data include extensive "photo identification" photography. I took all of the photos in this book on the "Enchanted River," except the picture labeled, 'Vidalia during his Rescue;' our thanks to Dr. Randy Wells, Chicago Zoological Society, for letting us include his photo. Dolphins share the seas with sharks, which we call "Mack the Knife," and encounters between them are reality. A disclaimer is that some stories may disturb young or sensitive readers.

I have exercised some artistic license. My research is conducted under federal research permits so I have changed the codes that identify individual dolphins to human names to introduce them on a first-name basis for this book. Each story also opens with a human parallel as a way to relate to what goes on at sea, but *I emphasize that dolphins think and act like dolphins. They are not people in dolphin suits.* Finally, dolphin bodies are very different than human bodies, so I have included a basic photo reference that identifies the names of their body parts used in these chapters.

Deep thanks to my thoughtful reviewers: Steve Goldberg; Maurine Morgan; Marc del Frate; Pat and Gary Hughes; Hollie Toppel; Marge, Mary, and Paul Weaver; John Heidemann; and the supportive staff at Jaasas Academic Press. I am deeply grateful to my editor Don Kerr for patiently nudging me away from the neutral technical writing of my scientific training towards prettier prose that sways to the rhythm of the sea itself.

One final note before storytelling: I once heard that the Inuit people of North America have 60 different words for snow, which means they see many different versions of it. Bottlenose dolphins are designed for social interaction, and we too see many different versions of it. These stories give but a glimpse of the depth and richness of their social lives at sea. Join me in marveling.

Ann Weaver, Ph.D., Animal Behaviorist (Ethologist)
Good-natured Statistics Consulting
Discreet and Friendly Data Handling Services – Even Friendlier Prices!
GoodNaturedStatistics.com

*National Oceanic and Atmospheric Administration (NOAA) permits 1088-1815, 16299, and 20346

***

"C'mon! It's a beautiful day at sea! Climb aboard and let's get on the water!"

Captain John adds, *"Brace yourself. This trip will be like nothing else in your life so far."*

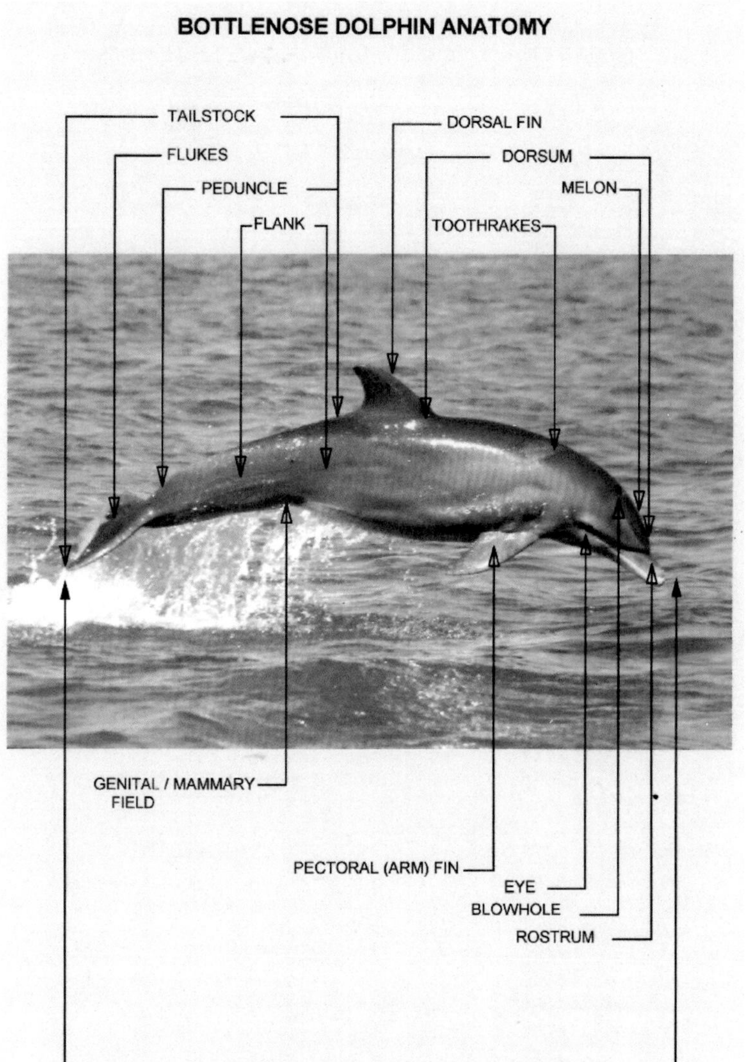

2. *Saga Dances with the Devil*

PHOTO BY ANN WEAVER, NOAA 16299-2, 6/10/2016

Saga's Deepest Shark Bites

***

Sharks and dolphins grow up together in the same saltwater nursery. Do sharks always attack dolphins or could some bites be accidental?

OUCH! Have you ever been physically assaulted when you least expected it and suffered the pain without knowing why it happened? That's exactly what happened one summer day to a young dolphin we call Saga.

That little dolphin reminded me of my big brother when we were kids. All youngsters stumble wide-eyed through a wonderland of discoveries anyway, but Saga was drawn more than most. He went faster and further than most, keeping his mom extra alert.

But if Saga approached the shark that day to play, we will never know.

On a calm summer morning in a shallow cove, Saga and his mom Sybil swam with friends Bette and her newborn, and a teenaged female. They poked around the hip-deep water along an undeveloped coastline, as Captain John and I have done many times. The shallows are safe, are they not? The three adults spread out to hunt. The two calves did not. Bette's baby was only 23 days old, a newborn glued to mom's side doing its best to breathe and swim. Saga was the other calf. Just a yearling living on mom's rich milk, he dallied at hunting.

Saga probably expected to play - like toddlers of all species: humans, dolphins, apes, monkeys, puppies, cubs, and kits. After all, he had spent his whole life playing. Plus, he was a year old now - the most playful time at sea. Who was around to play with?

Suddenly Saga shot out of the water frantically, dropped back in, and shot out explosively a second time. Water erupted behind him as something large and hidden shoved a giant splash sideways. The water exploded again, this time Saga cutting a wild zigzag of small white splashes as he frantically tried to dodge the immense fans of water zigzagging right behind him.

Five gray fins galloped out of the shallows into deeper waters, where they were met halfway by a quartet of incoming dolphins. They gathered together into a 2-ton (1800 kg.) wad of dolphin muscle and sprinted to the other side of the bay where they finally stopped and writhed around each other in wild excitement.

Suddenly, a massive new dorsal fin glinted among them. Had the shark followed them? I craned for clues. No! It was the big male Xavier, yet another dolphin attracted to the hubbub.

Every combination of the ten agitated dolphins surfaced together at different intervals, as if everyone checked in with everyone else. I was trying to track the ten briskly milling gray bodies – we did not yet know what happened – and caught my breath at glimpses of pink on small Saga.

Pink is the color of dolphin flesh beneath gray skin. Pink is the color of a fresh shark bite. Pink is Mack the Knife's calling card.

The ten agitated dolphins eventually calmed down and gradually parted company. The dolphins who raced to Saga's rescue headed south, three bulls irresistibly following their fetching female deep in one of her fertile phases.

Saga and schoolmates headed north. First Bette, her baby, and the teen set off rhythmically. Sybil trailed them with her little wounded son at her side. Poor Saga! Bitten or not, he had to keep swimming. Did he whimper-whistle in pain or stay silent?

***

Over the next several weeks, he poured his resources into healing. He became thin and sunken. He swam tentatively the way someone who uses a cane walks tentatively. Always at his side, his mom Sybil matched his painful pace.

Shark bites on dolphins are not always obvious at first. Time sometimes reveals more as the healing process turns slit dolphin skin white and the wounded dolphin becomes less skittish. Due to the whitening process, Saga looked worse two weeks later than when it first happened.

Saga's Deepest Shark Bites Three Weeks Later

***

Time eventually revealed that Saga had been bitten nine times – surely no accidental encounter in a mutual underwater feeding frenzy. Some bites were apparently glancing blows, mere seaside paper cuts. Others cut deep. The shark left its deepest impression on Saga's right side: 3 grisly U-shaped cuts from the shark's rounded jaws. Another slice on the top of Saga's tailstock stripped back a tab of skin like peeling a potato. Other bites lower on his body glinted below the water surface.

We will never know if Saga approached that shark as a potential playmate - like an inquisitive child reaching innocently for the flame. One wonders what kind of lesson he learned.

***

Clues about the natural relationship between dolphins and sharks are few and far between. Our observation of this encounter provided a few conclusions.

For example, the shark chased Saga, who zigzagged madly to escape it the way a fish zigzags madly to escape a feeding dolphin. Saga's mom Sybil rushed to Saga's side and with him fled the shark at top speed, shoving her son into deeper waters by skimming through the water surface. Their three schoolmates sped away with them, but the shark did not switch to the easier target of Bette's tiny newborn.

As Sybil bolted out of the shallows, half shoving and half dragging Saga with her, five new dolphins rushed over to help. Together they enveloped the wounded calf in a protective shield and escorted him away at speed. The incoming dolphins recognized what was happening. Observations like this argue that bottlenose dolphins recognize distress in others – as most mammals do. However, some passing dolphins also stopped to help – which most mammals, and many humans, do not.

We cannot say if the shark chased them after that first wild zigzag out of the immediate area or, if so, how far. However, judging from the distance to the spot where they stopped and milled feverishly, the shark did not follow them for long or at all. Their collective bulk probably discouraged it from further treachery, which implicates a more grisly outcome, had fewer dolphins been involved.

The dolphins milled around in agitation for some minutes after the event but then calmed down, formed their original groups, and went their separate ways. This suggested that the threat was over and that the shark did not stalk the wounded calf. Sybil and Saga swam away very slowly, trailing their schoolmates. Nothing in their pace said they fled a threat.

Finally, the shark did not repeat its attack although it had an easy target once the dolphins split up.

***

The relationship between sharks and dolphins on the "Enchanted River" is shrouded in mystery. When I see a dolphin with more than one shark bite scar, I wonder if it received all of the bites in a single intentional attack or as a series of accidental nips across the years in the same feeding frenzy in the inky blackness of night. Saga's dance with the devil pitches the pendulum toward intentional attack - nine bites in one encounter! His scars will be visible for the rest of his life.

Note, in this case the shark did not rip out huge chunks of dolphin flesh.

From what little is known, shark-dolphin interactions are neither robotic nor predictable. A grisly exception is that the sharks of the "Enchanted River" are much given to grabbing baby dolphins by the head. However! They also grab adult dolphins by the head - including our biggest bulls! What kind of psychology is involved in confronting a shark head-on?

Dolphin moms pay close attention to their calves. For example, they are very picky about their calf's playmates, stopping their child from playing with schoolmates whom they deem unsuitable. Yet some calves *are* bitten by sharks. Does that mean their mothers are inattentive? Maybe. On the other hand, if mom dolphins are just as picky and vigilant about sharks as they are about their calf's playmates, this would explain why we see so *few* calves with shark bite scars and why calf survival rates on the "Enchanted River" are so high (70%, based on 137 births).

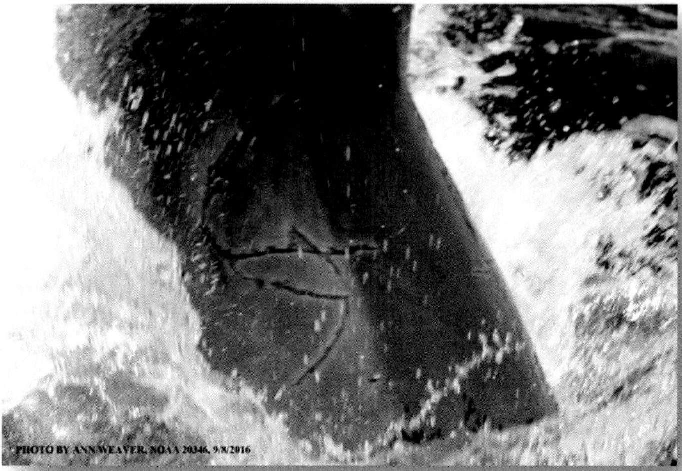

Saga's Scars Three Months Later

***

The dolphins' collective protection may have been inherited from ancestral relatives that evolved into two lines: today's whales, dolphins, and porpoises (cetaceans) and a large family of animals including cattle, pigs, deer, hippos, and musk ox (even-toed hoofstock). Specifically, sperm whales and musk ox form protective barriers around their young, the way Saga's rescuers formed a protective barrier around him. The dolphins did not mob the shark, the way for example song birds mob a crow to protect their young.

Our human interactions with predators appear to be similar to the dolphins'. Like them, we often succumb to attack. If we are fortunate or strong enough, we fight and survive with lessons learned; however, others around us may protect us. Hopefully these encounters teach us to recognize a threat to others and help them. Are these split-second actions of assistance based upon individual familiarity and devotion, or are they part of a cohesive societal ethic?

***

Saga's mother, Sybil, played a big role in his dramatic dance with the devil. This was not her first drama with one of her kids.

3. Burning Bonds of Love

Sybil Nudges her Little Dead Newborn Baby Floating on its Side

***

No parent should outlive their child. For a human parent, that loss is one of the most tragic and mind-changing episodes anyone can endure.

On land, we each handle the loss of a loved one in our own way. No one practices for it. No one is good at mourning. Some people manage to hide their grief; however, in others grief is agonizingly apparent.

At sea this is true too, and became terribly clear one gripping day eight years before Saga escaped a shark with the help of his mom Sybil and others.

Near sunset one spring day, Sybil's newborn launched his tiny shiny body over the water surface and plopped back down on his chin in the clumsy way of all newborn dolphins, the way a newborn human nods helplessly until his muscles gain control. The newborn, safely tucked between his mother Sybil and older brother Steve, slid and plopped with them through still waters.

The next day, the seas were calm and crystalline under the noon sun. The exposed sandbars of the three mangrove isles inside of The Pass connecting the Gulf of Mexico and Intracoastal Waterway were packed with anchored boats and recreational boaters. On the middle isle, 32 boats were anchored near two giant construction barges, each half the length of a football field, like junkyard cars jammed around rusty semi-trailers. None of the beaming boaters seemed to realize that the nearby group of eight dolphins was acting strangely. It was just as well. It was a gripping scene.

New mom Sybil slowly wove around a small area, her son Steve and five junior bulls jostling around her in great excitement. They blocked our view of her, so it took us a while to decide that something strange was indeed floating in front of her face, as limp as a flag in a slow wind.

Aww. It was her newborn baby. Dead.

Sybil kept nudging the body of her newly-dead baby with her head, keeping herself between the baby and young bulls who trailed her as breathless pairs or trios. When they flanked her, she would heave up and dive with force, straining to submerge while holding the corpse in her mouth. She did this as long as we could stand watching.

The wrenching scene of a mother dolphin futilely nudging the bobbing corpse of her dead baby makes it painful to remember 18th century economist Thomas Malthus' thesis: The business of nature is to produce far more individuals than the environment can sustain. A good example is the millions of acorns produced by an oak tree. Most acorns never become trees; else oak trees would cover the earth. Instead acorns feed countless animals. This is what we mean by the web of life.

Malthus cited plenty of ways to dispatch nature's excess – disease, pestilence, famine, predators. I eyed the glut of bulls milling breathlessly around Sybil and the bobbing corpse of her dead baby. Were they responsible, like tomcats killing kittens on the farm? Alternatively, these dolphins all knew each other well. Were they drawn to Sybil's struggles out of curiosity or, like elephants, out of compassion?

It is not puzzling that Sybil still attempted to mother her dead baby. Such behavior would be helpful if a calf swam abnormally because it was disabled or injured, just as it helped eight years later when it saved her future son Saga from a shark.

In a most stirring demonstration of what goes on in a mourning mother dolphin, Sybil did not give up the body of her dead baby for a week. Burning with single-minded motherhood, she continued to struggle to elicit a response from its indifferent corpse. It took that long to burn away the bond that tied her to him.

At first her behavior barely changed. But her companions did. Her son Steve remained in the vicinity, no longer swimming excitedly with a group of male teenage friends but now meandering nearby with a female friend. Sybil let them approach the corpse as they would. But when any other dolphins approached, she quickened and shoved the corpse away from them.

Slowly her behavior began to change. Naturally, she became hungry. Some days after the death, she went from constant contact with the corpse to leaving it for a moment to catch a quick bite to eat. But the indifferent corpse did not instinctively swim in a circle until she returned. She would rush back to it, but when it did not swim naturally alongside her, Sybil could only nudge it over and over with her face.

Sybil also felt the tug of life before the death. She would swim a short distance away with her son and schoolmate, leaving the bobbing corpse behind her. But, oh, that bond still burned. She wouldn't be a boat length away before hurrying back to it. Her son and schoolmate would keep going but presently return and repeat the routine again. That bond was scorching.

It burned through sometime after a week. As if complicit, the sea breeze held a tinge of smoke from far-away Florida fires.

***

Sybil's Terrible Skin Condition after the Death of her Baby

***

Poor Sybil! The next time we saw her after the death of her newborn, she had developed the worst case of dolphin dermatitis ever seen on the "Enchanted River." Covering her entire body, it took six months to heal. The cause of her dermatitis - whether bacterial, viral, or psychological - remains unknown. One possibility is that she was very depressed and stopped grooming.

We need to know much more about dolphin dermatitis, especially as humanity continues to pressure natural populations into dirtier, noisier seas that are increasingly crowded with boats. Dermatitis may be a non-invasive way to realize dolphins are under stress.

Other dolphin mothers whose calves die show behavioral changes. These are harder to see than a skin condition because observers must know a dolphin's habits very well to recognize that a dolphin is behaving in an unusual way, quite possibly associated with mourning.

Here are just two striking examples. Recall Sybil's schoolmate in Saga's Dance with the Devil, the mother with the newborn. That was Bette. That newborn was her second calf. Bette was never much for surfing the wakes made by passing boats. Yet after the death of her first calf, she spent several months surfing every possible passing boat. When I told Barbara Brunnick about this, a marine mammalogist with forty years of experience, she said without hesitation, "Bette found a way to cope." Another mom, Diana, went from friendly with our boat to impossible to approach for months after her son Doodle's ghastly death from shark attack.

These and other observations show that some dolphins exhibit an immediate reaction to the death of certain dolphins but may also continue to respond to that death long after.

***

Why did Sybil's baby die? No one knows. It is one of many unsolved mysteries on the "Enchanted River." Newborn dolphins die for many unknown reasons. Like tomcats, should the jostling presence of junior bulls implicate them in the death of Sybil's baby? Male bottlenose dolphins (bulls) in other study areas have been accused of killing calves, the dark behavior called infanticide. The presence of bulls with a female shortly after her calf's death raises this thorny possibility. But as any attorney will argue, proximity is only circumstantial evidence. Moreover, female dolphins on the "Enchanted River" who lose their calf to a shark are also soon accompanied by bulls. Bulls are bloodhounds when it comes to locating newly available females - though we cannot say if it is the mother's cries or chemistry that draws them. Finally, the bulls in our study site rarely treat calves roughly; in fact, most are gentle or playful.

Little wonder Sybil was affected by the loss of her newborn. The behaviors of a mammal mother and her baby are elegantly designed to fit together like two sides of a zipper.

In addition, bottlenose dolphin mothers are the most visibly affectionate animal mothers I have ever seen. On the "Enchanted River," a mother dolphin and her calf have stayed together as long as eight years, and reunite periodically for years after the calf has grown and left to live independently. This demonstrates a powerful bond that goes far beyond the reflexes of instinct.

*****

4. *Dolphin Sense of Fair Play*

Simon Peers at the People in the Boat after Protecting his Friends' Babies from Intruders

***

Rules, rules, everywhere! Though it sometimes seems that there are too many, rules that govern our human societies give us a sense of order, purpose, and hopefully an ultimate sense of safety. What about at sea?

People the world over come to vacation along Florida's sugary-sandy coastlines, and most hope to see dolphins. Should you make the journey here, do spend time out on the water and enjoy the scenery. But follow the rules. Here's a little hint.

On a mid-summer day, three baby dolphins were playing with each other, their mouths wide open and their bodies jiggling through sparkling seas; I longed to somersault in gravity-free space like them.

A grinning couple on a jet ski floated next to the dolphin babies and savored the sight of their cheerful play. Entranced by the mesmerizing action, they did not notice that there were several adult dolphins nearby. Nor did they notice when the largest of the adults swam towards their jet ski with great purpose.

But they surely noticed when he surfaced next to them and slammed his massive tailstock on the water three thumping times, "Do YOU *MIND?* We have babies here!"

The tail-slapping dolphin, Simon, is not an argumentative bull by nature - quite the opposite. But in his view, the grinning couple on the jet ski moved too close to the playing baby dolphins. They violated his sense of space around the kids, which evidently irritated him enough to express himself clearly.

Simon is notably affectionate but otherwise unusual among the bottlenose bulls who navigate the "Enchanted River." For example, he works alone without an alliance partner or what I call a bonded bull buddy. Most bottlenose dolphin bulls here form deep bonds with one or more males; some bonds last for years or a lifetime. Bonded bull buddies can out-compete rivals, especially if rivals are lone bulls without a buddy, which puts lone bulls at a disadvantage. Yet not all bulls bond with another bull. Working alone does not seem to hinder Simon, which suggests that he has high social status. He is also rarely toothraked. Toothrakes come from teeth dragged along the dolphin skin, which dolphins do to each other for a variety of reasons, but definitely when they fight. That Simon is rarely toothraked also suggests his high social status because it implies that he gets his way without fighting. Even more distinctive is that Simon is so likely to be found with one or more of a half dozen lady dolphins in our study area that we have called these females "Simon's Sallies" for years. Bottlenose bulls in our study area do not form harems. So Simon and his Sallies are unusual in showing obvious preferences for one another. Finally, Simon really likes babies. The bulls of the "Enchanted River" are affectionate and playful with calves, but Simon is the most playful. Mother dolphins clearly trust him.

Simon Rears up over Two Calves in Play

***

On this lovely summer day, all three of the mother dolphins with Simon were "Simon's Sallies:" Courtney, Bette, and Lana. Based on the time they spent together the year before when the ladies became pregnant with their current calves, Simon is the likely father of Courtney's and Bette's yearling calves and is a possible father of Lana's tender month-old calf. Either way, they had known each other for years and definitely trusted Simon with their kids.

However, trusting your baby's father is a human concept. How would Simon know he is a calf's father? Presumably, he does not know who his offspring are, like most mammal males. In addition, he presumably has little or no concept of fatherhood itself. It seems to me that if bottlenose bulls had an idea of fatherhood, we would see them show paternal behavior. That is, they would act like fathers, such as swimming with their offspring regularly and keeping an eye out for them. To my eye, the bottlenose bulls in our study area do not act like this.

On the other hand, it is reasonable to expect that when Simon knows a calf's mother very well, he will share his affection with her baby too. That certainly goes for any baby of "Simon's Sallies."

The mesmerized couple on the jet ski understood Simon's message, backed off, and eventually wandered away. The dolphins headed in the opposite direction at a leisurely pace.

Under Captain John's silky piloting, we fell into step with them and entered that zone of serenity where relaxed dolphins send observers. The calves darted among the adults as they went, wrestling and surfacing erratically with that marvelous energy that makes fools of photographers who try to capture their zest in a picture.

Seeing Simon swim alongside his "Sallies" reminded me of many such companionable swims in years past. A decade of observations of this behavior suggests that friendship is a fair term for local bottlenose dolphins and, moreover, that they have long-term friendships. I also think it is fair to suggest they have a sense of trust, the flipside of which is mistrust.

In one of those few precious moments when I am not entering data or taking a photo, I recalled two other times when Simon clearly protected calves. In both cases, he protected them from dolphins rather than people on jet skis. Both rescues were dramatic and extraordinary because they involved rare behavior. One involved a kidnapping, told in story #5. The other involved a rare case of junior bulls harassing a baby. Simon intervened directly in both situations and freed the calf to race back to its mom.

Protection by itself is a form of sophisticated social behavior. It implies some understanding of what is happening to another individual and that intervention may resolve the threat. In addition, it may also involve recognizing that some rule of conduct has been violated. Watching the silky companionability of Simon and his Sallies made me wonder which is true: Does Simon only protect the calves of his female friends? Or does Simon move to protect any calf who, in his opinion, needs help? Evidence that Simon protected the calf of a female he does *not* know well suggests the stunning proposal that Simon has a sense of justice or fair play when it comes to vulnerable calves.

In both of Simon's dramatic and extraordinary calf rescues, I knew that neither mother of the rescued calf was a "Simon's Sally." I couldn't wait to see exactly what kind of relationships he did have with them.

Back at the lab, I dove into my database and swam around awhile. Based on a 13-year history of Simon's social encounters, he only had passing acquaintances with the two mothers whose calves he rescued so dramatically. That is, our records showed that he was only seen with those mothers as schoolmates a handful of times, including the day of his dramatic rescue. There cannot be much of a relationship between individuals who rarely spend time together.

Big beautiful Simon, who works alone, rarely fights, and likes kids, seems to have a great generosity of spirit to match. Intervening not only for babies of friends but also of strangers suggests that when it comes to babies Simon has a sense of justice. The next story shows how he shows it.

5. Clara the Kidnapper and Simon the Savior

Clara's Tactic for Keeping her Baby at her Side

***

You are standing in line at the store with your baby behind you in a stroller while you pay your bill. You turn to collect your baby and the stroller is gone!

Mid-summer after bridge construction finally ended, we kept spotting two inseparable dolphin moms sprinting around the "Enchanted River," each with a small calf. We knew them from periodic sightings before bridge construction began but had not seen them since. They were very difficult to approach. Their galloping flights went beyond protective maternal departures.

As always when I see skittish dolphins like this, I wondered why they behave as they do.

In contrast to the skittish dolphins, local lady Clara strolled around her favorite bay one dewy morning in typical new mom style, ushering a small calf around the shallows. She had finally had another baby. It had been seven years, about twice as long as usual between babies for local females. We stayed at a distance to avoid pressuring her and the new baby – which, though it was very little, swam too well to be a newborn.

Oddly, another adult hovered near Clara and sometimes appeared to follow her hesitantly. I thought it was possibly Clara's previous now-grown calf Student, because an older sibling sometimes reappears with miraculous timing to meet their newborn sibling. But this adult stayed in the shadows that the low morning sun cast off the mangroves; I could not identify it in the shadows and might have to wait to see who it was by reviewing its pictures later back at the lab. I was acutely aware of not knowing the identity of the dolphin who hovered around Clara and her baby.

Then one of those spectacular assemblies began where more and more dolphins appear out of the blue as if drawn to something of seaside significance. As incoming dolphins approached from the north, Clara abruptly herded the calf in the opposite direction, south, an expected response for a new mom.

Yet the ensuing chaos was completely unexpected!

As we trailed Clara, the incoming dolphins began streaming by us at speed, heading in the same direction as Clara had taken her calf. Nick, one of the incoming dolphins, shot past the boat in a quick greeting and caught up to Clara in a rush. Together they swept the new baby behind an island into a sheltered basin we call "The Bathtub."

Another nine dolphins streamed by our boat in a long line, also heading for The Bathtub. We paused and took their pictures as they swept by (five females and bulls Simon, Bruce, Drake, and Rick).

Two more massive bulls steamed by, Gil and Ted, and swung by the boat briefly. Gil surged at our bow, displaying strange new marks on his back like a grilled hot dog and breathing hard enough to dose me with his DNA from his wet exhalation.

We headed to The Bathtub too, where milling dolphins were joined by more and more dolphins that swirled in from out of nowhere. A mother dolphin galloped around with her small calf in the distance, which I assumed was one of the two inseparable visiting moms we had spotted galloping around The Pass lately. I momentarily wondered how easily these rare visitors socialized with the resident dolphins. I knew that one of them, Law, was familiar with many of the dolphins on scene today, but not with resident dolphins Clara or Simon, which would be notable later.

Dolphins swirled wildly around The Bathtub for half an hour. Captain John maneuvered brilliantly, but confusion reigned. Dolphins burst out here and there like popcorn in a wind tunnel. What animated them so? It wasn't food; nothing edible appeared on sonar. Newborns rarely create this kind of excitement. Perhaps there were some fertile females that provoked the bulls into *stylin'* for them, and everyone else was watching like spectators in seaside bleachers, but if so it was not obvious to us.

Suddenly, Simon the bull dolphin acted decisively. He is rarely roused to wrath or anything else that requires big energy. But he arched his massive body over the water surface and launched aggressively into the galloping mother-calf pair whose identity he obliterated in his explosive take-down. Confusion still reigned. Dolphins darted everywhere. Clara rushed out of the fray, the calf at her side, along with a second adult dolphin who also stuck to her like glue. I now recognized the second adult as one of the two inseparable mothers, Law.

All of the dolphins disappeared under the surface.

When they finally emerged again, they had all spread out and were leaving in different directions. The drama was over.

Reunited, the two inseparable dolphin moms galloped westward with their small calves toward a mangrove isle where they established themselves a good distance from the remaining dolphins but, notably, not out of earshot. We approached them carefully and took photo documentation pictures of both mothers with their calves.

The remaining dolphins streamed eastward and slowly calmed down, their untidy milling eventually switching to tranquil socializing. Bruce and Drake resumed their celebrated vigil next to Faye, who is the hero in the next story. Rick extended excited invitations to his favorite females Sabine and Bette. Simon vanished. Clara was nowhere to be found.

But we found her the next day. She did not have a calf.

***

The wild excitement we had witnessed was because Clara had evidently kidnapped another mother's baby - a one-time event during 13 years of study along the "Enchanted River." Our photos showed that the dolphin who hovered around Clara throughout the entire episode was the calf's mother, Law, and the kidnapped calf was hers. Other dolphins heard the hubbub and, like people rushing over and crowding around a dramatic event, rushed over to see what all the excitement was about. As the seaside spectators rushed after Clara, she rushed away from them, keeping the helpless calf at her side in the ensuing hubbub.

As Clara rushed away with the kidnapped calf, the calf's mother joined the incoming dolphins, many of whom she knew from years before. They dashed after Clara collectively and swirled around them in great excitement.

Finally, big bull Simon intervened by crashing into Clara, releasing the calf she kidnapped, and allowing its frantic mother to rush in and reunite with her baby. The next day, Law and her baby left the "Enchanted River," returning only twice in the next four years.

***

What are the triggers that provoke an individual into kidnapping? In the dolphin world there are no financial rewards to be gained from a ransom. Is it a sense of jealousy, wanting something someone else has?

As it turned out, Clara was two months pregnant when she kidnapped Law's baby. According to our records, she had not had a calf in seven years. Did Clara "kidnap" Law's baby for innocent reasons to practice motherhood?

Simon saved the kidnapped calf this day, playing the role of a policeman. Overall, though, he has little opportunity to show this stirring behavior because the dolphin babies of the "Enchanted River" are seldom mistreated. Little opportunity is true of the next story too.

6. A Dolphin First Responder

PHOTO BY ANN WEAVER, Ph.D., NOAA 1088-1815, 10/3/2004

Valiant Writhing in Pain from a Fresh Shark Bite

***

If you were bit by a shark, you would leave the water as soon as you could – right?

Few of us have the courage to assist someone who is in peril, especially if it endangers our own lives, and we justifiably call those with the courage heroes. Professionals who put themselves in peril for others and are the first on the scene are known as "first responders," heroes willing to sacrifice it all to come to the aid of others.

One warm, crystal blue autumn day, we were exploring the nooks and crannies of the "Enchanted River," hoping to find enough dolphins to justify a study. Pilot work like this is pleasant, like thinking about Christmas in November. It is full of promise.

Our reverie was shattered when we came upon a mother dolphin who had *just* been bitten by a shark. Writhing in pain, she slammed herself against the water surface the way a person beats their headache against a pillow. She corkscrewed round and round her young calf, the way a person in pain seeks contact comfort. Despite the painful effort it involved, she did endless headstands, elevating her tailstock over the surface as if she could not bear the sting of the salt water.

The writhing dolphin's fresh shark bite was a big ghoulish "grin" of sliced skin on the left side of her tailstock. It did not bleed. Instead it filled with blubber, a kind of biological first aid kit. Dolphin blubber is as elastic as chewing gum. In emergencies, it swells to fill gaps and seals off any tendency to bleed - a handy feature for animals who swim naked among sharks. Blubber also stretches like chewing gum pulled into strings. Strings of blubber flapped off the writhing mother's fresh wound like tatters on an old flag.

If "Mack the Knife" - the shark that bit the mother dolphin - was still around, it contacted the writhing mom and calf no more. It had made its point, whatever that was.

We found the dolphin with a shark bite a few days later and considered her survival most valiant. So that is why we called her Valiant. We called her baby Vic. Still in pain and moving slowly, she and Vic were swimming with a local lady dolphin we call Faye.

A regular sight on the "Enchanted River," Faye is a resident dolphin. She is very social, often on the edge of other dolphins' activities like a mom watching faithfully from the bleachers. She is a good mom, too. She taught me that mother dolphins teach their young calves how far to stay from our often-intrusive boat.

Remarkably, Faye is also the one who is most likely to swim with dolphins with new shark bites - a kind of seaside "first responder."

It took me years to realize this because shark bites are infrequent in our study area. Faye was the first dolphin we saw with Valiant after the latter's brutal bite. It was not until two summers later that Faye had her next chance to exhibit the same behaviour again. After Lana's son was chomped on the tail like Valiant was, and Sybil's son Steve was bit on his shoulder,

Faye was among the first we saw to swim with them both. She also swam with a dolphin called Michigan that summer, further evidence of Faye's first responder behavior in that she only swam with that poor shark-magnet dolphin one other time ever.

The next summer, we found Bette limp-swimming with a fresh shark bite on her back. The shark's teeth marks were plain to see. Strings of blubber flowed off the wound. Again Faye was there, matching Bette's painful pace.

Happily, each of these wounded dolphins survived. How many shark-bitten dolphins survive because of the presence of other dolphins?

Bottlenose dolphins have a long scorecard of being helpful and unselfish. For example, during history's bloody days when men harpooned dolphins the same way they harpoon whales, dolphin schoolmates propped up injured dolphins between them and carried them away. In like manner, bottlenose dolphins help newborns to the water surface to breathe at birth and form large protective clusters around young calves. They also intervene for calves, related or not. They surround a dolphin who is being bitten by a shark and shepherd it away with collective bulk, likely discouraging the shark in the process. Even human history is dotted with miraculous moments when dolphins helped by taking a person to shore or warding off sharks. In several parts of the world, wild dolphins even gather and *share* their fish with people.

This kind of generosity – empathy - has to start with individual dolphins who recognize that someone else needs help. But they must also be willing to provide help, from psychological support to putting themselves at potential risk. Faye is one of them. I feel honored to know her.

***

While Faye hovered around Bette and her new shark bite, Faye's little calf Babyface zipped around them both. Faye's vigil with her wounded friend exposed her vulnerable calf and herself to danger IF the shark that bit Bette was still hanging around and skulking at the edges of the gloom. Anyone would think it unwise to let a baby zip around when there are sharks in the area. My observations of behavior like this suggest that sharks on the "Enchanted River" do not hang around dolphins after they bite them.

It is easy to assume that sharks attack and kill dolphins, rushing in to rip out a brutal hunk of flesh and retreating to wait for death. The sharks and dolphins of the "Enchanted River" have a profound story – too long for this book. All I will say for now is that sharks do not kill dolphins on the "Enchanted River."

*****

**** Seaside Showmanship ****

7. *Dying for Attention*

PHOTO BY ANN WEAVER, Ph.D., NOAA 16299, 4/1/2014

The Grisly Site of a Dolphin Floating Lifelessly

***

How far will you go to make an impression?

Drastic action is sometimes required in order to attract someone's attention. People employ various physical methods, such as altering clothing, hair style, furniture, or vehicles to impress others. Since dolphins have none of these at hand, they have found several different methods to make their point.

No one is surprised to hear that mothers invest great energy, affection, and care in their babies. That goes for dolphins too. No one should be surprised to hear that males invest great energy, affection, and care into courtship; this investment goes for dolphins too. Yet one winter day, something happened that showed the kind of thought that some bottlenose bulls put into courtship.

Male and female bottlenose dolphins of the "Enchanted River" do not marry. But they 'go steady' after a fashion when seen together over the course of several consecutive months or years. For example, bonded bull buddies Bruce and Drake invested many months courting Queen Priscilla over a two-year period. One day towards the end of that run, they had added competition for her attention from two other bulls. This evidently called for drastic action.

Captain John and I were still at the dock when a dolphin sextet swam past and were soon out of sight. We rushed to launch and headed in their direction.

We found the attractive Queen Priscilla, her older calf Paisley, and four male suitors in a broad bay. As is typical of groups where several males vie for the attention of a technically available female, the dolphins milled around a great deal. Milling makes it hard for researchers to figure out what is going on.

Another reason it was hard to figure out what was going on was that Priscilla's calf Paisley was darting around like a crazy lady. She was still in her mother's care but almost five years old. Untried females like her are of no interest to courting bulls, who ignore their shy invitational gestures with behavior we call *"Little Girls, Keep Out!"*

In contrast, untried females like Paisley are interested in bulls, though shyly. Today Paisley tried to weave around them while they tried to weave around her mother. This added to the confusion.

An attractive female sparks male rivalry. Sexually-inclined dolphins of both sexes often float on their sides or backs at the water surface to invite some quality attention. Such invitations are brief because someone usually accepts the floating dolphin's invitation, pushing it up from underneath or pushing it down by swimming over it.

One of the dolphins began floating on its back like a person in a reclining chair, its chin poking out. I started taking pictures to be ready if its floating behavior ended in a mount, which I expected it to do. There was no telling who the dolphin was because only its chest and chin were visible, and I normally need to see a dorsal fin from the side to identify a dolphin. So we watched in anticipation without knowing who was floating there.

Reclining, the floating dolphin's blowhole was in the water. The floating dolphin was holding its breath.

The other five dolphins reacted bizarrely. Each in turn swam over the floating dolphin slowly, moving across its belly so that they momentarily formed the shape of a cross. Rare for rivalry, these swim-overs were not excited sexual mount attempts. Instead, they were done slowly, almost hesitantly. The floating dolphin never moved. Each dolphin returned and hesitantly repeated the crisscross gesture.

The floating dolphin did not move for half a minute, a lifetime at sea. Two dolphins moved behind it and nudged its head with their chins, a rare gesture. Others gently nudged the floating dolphin's belly with their chins. Because this tickles, we expected the floating dolphin to spring into action.

Still it did not move. I was just lowering my camera to watch it closely as Captain John warned, "There might be something wrong with that dolphin."

Was it dying? I had watched a dolphin slowly die one sobering afternoon years before, an experience I did not want to repeat.

The five other dolphins kept swimming over and nudging the floating dolphin hesitantly. Still it neither moved nor breathed. No longer reclining, it floated frankly on its back, its white belly staring at the winter sky like a dead fish.

By now the dolphin had been floating lifelessly for over a minute, an eternity at sea. By process of elimination, we realized it was dear Drake who floated lifelessly. My heart sank. I was not ready to say goodbye to this pillar of local dolphin society.

We kept staring. The dolphins kept nudging. Time slowed like Einstein said it does.

***

Death often involves spasms. Drake's head bobbed up at the surface, just like the dying dolphin had done to heave its last breath before it sank forever.

But in toe-curling slow motion Drake inched forward as if he was straining to do a sit-up and then a somersault, gradually revealing the long length of his powerful body and muscular tailstock – which he then lifted up and slammed down on the water surface with a resounding smack to punctuate his dramatic invitation!

Lifeless no more, this bull illusionist smacked the water again for good measure – triumphantly, I guess – having used his dramatic gesture to rivet everyone's attention on him.

We had never seen anything like it before. From their responses, I do not think the other dolphins had either.

***

The competition among four bulls for Priscilla's attention evidently called for drastic action, to which Drake responded by generating his outstanding "dying for attention" display.

But, dolphin-like, there was another surprise. Priscilla was already three months pregnant. Why would bulls bother to vie for the attention of a female who was already pregnant, unless relationships at sea mean more than simple sex?

***

The next story also shows that, sometimes, sex at sea is no simple matter.

*****

8. Sylvia's High Flying Romance

Sylvia Defies Gravity

***

Have you ever shown off on the dance floor? Did it work?

Occasionally it can be of great advantage for us to go beyond our every day actions or ability and push our normal physical limits to gain attention, especially if potential romance is involved.

Laughing and clinking glasses, people standing on a square dock at a congenial cocktail party congratulated themselves one December day for spending their Christmas holiday in those warm "winter" days of Florida.

As if planned for their pleasure, a dolphin leapt out of the water magnificently near their comfortable viewing stage. The cocktail crowd shrieked.

Then the dolphin leapt again. And again. The crowd roared. *Wow!* What a sparkling show!

The dolphin's beautiful leaps and splashes were an elaborate improvisation with brilliant flourishes, but its *cadenza* was not a trained dolphin act put on for the benefit of the cocktail crowd. It was natural dolphin showmanship – one way that one dolphin uses to attract another dolphin's attention. But why tell that to the cocktail crowd and spoil their life-long memory of a cherished Florida event?

We could have told the cocktail crowd all about this striking event. An hour before, Captain John and I were running the southern leg of our dolphin survey route when we spied a far-away dolphin. It led to an observation of unparalleled athleticism that had all the elements of field work the way a great holiday has all the elements of a great vacation.

A great holiday has leisure. Our fieldwork's version of leisure is patience. Today's dolphins required more patience than usual to approach and identify. They covered great distances of water between surfacing to breathe. We would see a dolphin near the shoreline. Then we would see a dolphin in the middle of the bay a football field away. These types of observations sometimes mean that there are several dolphins in the area and sometimes that only one dolphin is darting around madly. Either way, swift and unseen long-distance sorties like this exasperate researchers and boat captains alike.

Nonetheless, Captain John navigated with admirable ease over the many minutes it took us to establish that there were two dolphins. One was teen female Sylvia. The other was teen male Puck. They were an example of dolphins who were raised in the same waters at the same time but who did not know each other growing up, like kids from two different neighborhoods. Puck had matured extraordinarily early and weaned from his stately mother, Queen Priscilla, at the remarkably young age of sixteen months. He not only survived, he flourished. Our records suggested Sylvia and Puck were new acquaintances.

They hunted separately but within audio contact of each other. Hunting dolphins cover acres of aquatic territory anyway. But these teens were at the height of their physical powers - the fleetest dolphins of all.

A great holiday involves unexpected invitations. Field work's version is flexibility. Abruptly, their hunt was over. In splendid coordination they left their respective bays, surfaced next to each other, and trotted away some distance to a hidden cove that would become Sylvia's private stage.

Of course, holidays involve extra snacking. Field work's version is dolphins who find seaside snacks along the way. In the hidden cove, the two teens worked together to snare a few final fish snacks. At the height of their physical powers, they opted for snacks that required them to sprint down the entire length of the cove in a showy surge, although one wonders if that level of energetic expression was absolutely necessary.

Hopefully, a great holiday involves flirting, if not romance. It was time to alternate feeding (the world's oldest behavior) with the world's other oldest behavior, or at least its preliminaries. They started flirting.

Puck started it with a warm session of gentle shove swimming. This is when dolphins swim side by side and nudge each other with the part of their body that eons ago used to be a shoulder. This position puts them eye-to-eye in what we on the "Enchanted River" call the *intimate distance.* Gentle shouldering gave way to pressing against each other and rolling sideways. Or, one dolphin would draw itself along the entire length of the other dolphin's body, caressing without hands. Only humans relish such long sweeps of bodily contact as much.

Puck continued to weave around Sylvia warmly. He stroked her belly with his head. He swam over her. Sometimes he followed close behind her, sometimes she him, all in a gentle waltz.

Other than the one time that Sylvia snatched a fish next to the boat like a dancer dashing behind the curtain to pop an hors d'oeuvre into her mouth before springing back on stage, their affectionate choreography went on for many minutes. The clinking cocktail crowd had not yet noticed.

The Christmas holiday involves kissing under the mistletoe. Puck moved to mount. Sylvia slid out from under him, leaving him to an ungallant belly flop. He arched over the water in a splashy pounce. She sprang higher, then threw herself in the air like falling backwards onto a trampoline, her pectoral (arm) fins wide open. She landed with a whoosh, rolled on her side, and floated in dolphin invitation.

Sylvia Warms Up by Falling Backward as if on a Trampoline

***

Just as dancing can be part of a Christmas party, Sylvia became more and more animated. After Puck's belly flop, she graduated from popping half her body vertically out of the water in "mere" spyhops to her first grand leap – which was what started the cocktail crowd shrieking at the start of our story. Her leaps became fancier until she was doing twisting back flips!

She leapt and spun and twisted again and again in the most vivacious display of aerial behavior seen to date. By now she had the cocktail crowd riveted.

But her graceful displays of athleticism were about Puck. Her leaps were for him. She landed each display near him, impressively washing walls of water over him without touching him. Then she slid back into the water like a ballerina performing a single elegant point. Puck was presumably riveted too.

Sylvia's Back Flips with a Twist

***

She leapt and slid back in. He pounced. She leapt and slid back in. He pounced. They rolled with open mouths.

Her utter physical control was pure chic in action. I clicked my camera with greed. The cocktail crowd kept shrieking.

Any great holiday ends too soon, as does our field work. With signature suddenness, Puck and Sylvia surfaced side by side like normal dolphins do. Then they were gone.

***

Any behavior in which much or all of the dolphin's body comes out of the water is called an aerial behavior. Dolphins often do aerials when helping perpetuate their species, sometimes leaping to avoid unsuitable suitors and other times, like Sylvia, leaping to attract suitable ones.

Sylvia's Elegant Ballerina Spyhops

***

But her display was only one of many different "attitudes behind the aerials." Dolphins leap out of the water when they are flirting, playing, surfing, greeting, trying to remove cleaner fish called remoras, and especially when they are fighting. When a dolphin jumps out of the water, it can take a long time to explain why, if at all.

***

The art of seduction crosses many lines of conduct; this case was a beautiful example of getting it right. Sylvia was very excited to be with Puck. Her athletic display this day remains unparalleled in its enthusiasm and style.

But the dolphins of the "Enchanted River" are generally enthusiastic about displaying their endurance, athletic ability, and even unsuspected social skills to reap the desired reward, as the next story demonstrates.

*****

9. Shall We Dance?

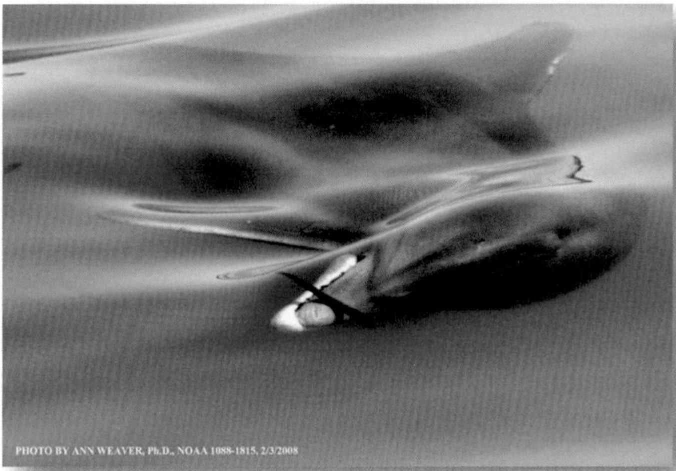

Scrapefin Sam Prepares to Flip a Mangrove Seed "Horsetail" into the Sky

***

Bonded bull buddies are stunningly cooperative with each other – even when it comes to romance.

On some occasions, personality alone is not enough to attract the attention we want. It can be helpful to employ props or unusual actions to demonstrate our prowess and accomplish our objectives.

One December day, Scrapefin Sam and his bonded bull buddy Ski leisurely rounded a watery corner and came across some drifting horsetails, mangrove seedpods that look like green-brown pencils.

Local dolphins sometimes throw horsetails around. Horsetail tossing is neat to see because the dolphins lunge out of the water to do so and lucky observers can see more of them. Dolphins toss horsetails for different reasons: to play a game, to reduce tension in social circumstances, and to attract attention.

For some reason the two bulls today found the horsetails particularly exciting. They suddenly sprung into action the way a person leaps to life when they realize the need to buy a last-minute Christmas present!

They separated some thirty feet apart and started throwing horsetails around.

Usually only one dolphin in a group tosses a horsetail. So this episode of horsetail tossing was more interesting because both bulls tossed horsetails.

Incredibly, they also *coordinated* their exhibition by tossing their horsetails in alternate order. Sam grabbed a horsetail in his mouth, whipped it high into the sky, and lunged after it with dramatic flair. Then Ski stabbed the sky with his projectile the same way. Then Sam stabbed the sky with his. Then Ski again. Then Sam again, this time pouncing on his horsetail next to the boat in mock attack and then zooming up to it from below, looking through the water to see if we were watching, which of course we were.

Was this striking display of coordinated team-tossing a simple case of maritime tomfoolery? If not, why did they do it?

The likely reason why they did it sped up in short order: Sabine. We had just left an observation of her in her luncheon bay and knew she had swiftly covered a mile of water to join these bulls – good buddies of hers, especially Sam.

***

Whether the bulls' team-tossing was just a game of agility for players and spectators to enjoy or an incredible and pretty bid for the lady's attention, the three dolphins leisurely rounded the next watery corner side-by-side. The horsetails returned to their drifting.

PHOTO BY ANN WEAVER, Ph.D., NOAA 1088-1815, 12/19/2007

Scrapefin Sam Stabs the Sky with his Horsetail

***

Some potential bids for the attention of other dolphins are surprisingly indirect, as in the next story.

*****

10. Legendary Lust or Fair is Fair?

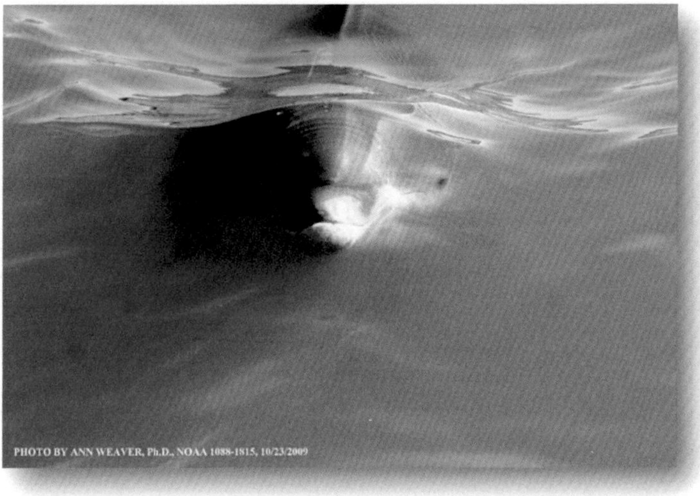

PHOTO BY ANN WEAVER, Ph.D., NOAA 1088-1815, 10/23/2009

Celine Visits the Boat before her Lesson in Fair Play

***

It took courage for young David to take on the giant Goliath.

Perception of our surroundings and potential threats to us or our loved ones is a basic animal instinct that assures our survival. Yet our perception of danger may be wrong and we have to rely on others to make the right call.

Without warning, the two big bulls were pouncing on the two-year-old as if to see which bull could dunk the calf first.

A fourth dolphin torpedoed in, swept the calf into its protective jet stream, and shepherded it to safety many feet away.

The calf innocently rushed back to the bulls like a horse rushing back into a burning barn, three separate times. The calf was having fun.

Each time, her rescuer rushed to her aid, only to be dunked for its efforts.

Ultimately, the solution sped by in the form of a fabulous yacht. Three dolphins leapt into its fast-track wake to surf and were gone.

What just happened? It had started as an idyllic seaside scene in the cool waters of autumn. Young miss Celine was playing with teen Bette, the maritime counterpart to a five-year-old playing with a sixteen-year-old. Celine periodically breached to rid herself of a ticklish cleaner fish called a remora. Although Bette did not have a remora, she is a "jumpy" dolphin and companionably threw herself into the skies here and there as well. Between aerials, the girls galloped around together or paused for a good-natured wrestle. Celine's mom Celeste hunted nearby.[ii]

All this time, two senior bulls swam in their vicinity. They were presumably considering the possibilities presented by the calf's mother but had not put obvious moves on her.

The competition started to simmer when five junior bulls streamed in from the east.

Rick and Ski arrived first. Rick is a small but feisty male who is willing to take on any sized rival. Within months he would be Bette's most serious suitor. At this time Bette frequently sought his company, zooming over to him from out of nowhere with minor flirtations. (If they were people, we would say, "She liked him.")

The other three junior bulls pulled up a short time later: Scrapefin Sam, Vic, and Oliver. Vic and Oliver were very junior bulls at the time, so their trio was similar to two 14-year-old guys hanging around with a guy in his 20s. Scrapefin Sam was older and developing confidence (given that he was increasingly involved in conflicts) but was by no means a top gun.

None of the five junior bulls could individually win a clash with the two senior bulls. But dolphins can count well enough to respect the power of numbers, in this case, 5 against 2. However, they rely on more than pure muscle power.

The junior bulls knew Celine and Bette well and approached them directly in greeting. This evidently ignited tensions because all started milling around the way nervous people mill around – all but the calf's mother Celeste. She continued hunting nearby.

Sure enough, the bulls started to scuffle. Dolphin fights are the watery version of dogs trying to bite each other and horses trying to kick each other. Because dolphins fight in water, observers mostly see splashing with an occasional flying body part. True to form, the splashing obscured who was doing what to whom today.

The sudden scuffle was over in a moment. The waters calmed. The junior bulls sprinted to the sidelines, close enough to monitor the situation but far enough away to avert further attack. That was when the two senior bulls started pouncing on Celine, Bette came to her rescue, and with the calf's mother they ultimately caught the passing fast-track yacht out of town.

***

This observation was a notable form of self-expression for the same reason that the story of David and Goliath endures across time: A young adult female dared to rescue a calf from two bulls who outweighed her three-fold, and this is rare to see. But this dramatic rescue also has perplexing angles that suggest various interpretations.

One perplexing angle was that none of the seven bulls made sexual overtures to the females. This contradicts bottlenose dolphins' reputation for legendary lust, largely from captive dolphins engaging in recreational sex to the point of shameless promiscuity. But it fits with 13 years of observing dolphin recreational sex at sea as behavior that is doled out selectively among possible partners. Rather than a reflex, I submit that sex at sea involves a great deal of social maneuvering, although negotiation often just looks like a bunch of dolphins swimming around. With no sign of courtship today, why should we say the bulls were fighting over the females? If not over females, why fight?

More perplexing was that the two senior bulls pounced on the calf Celine. This is rare behavior in itself but seemed really out of context. Although the senior bulls won their short scuffle with the junior bulls, maybe they were still tense and pounced on the calf as tension release. Whatever the reason, Bette did not see it as fair, for it was she and not the calf's mom who rushed over to shepherd young Celine to safety.

Interventions like this raise the possibility that dolphins have rules of engagement. Rules can be violated, and violations may trigger a dolphin sense of fair play or justice. Maybe Bette thought that the bulls were pouncing too hard for a calf that age. Granted, dolphins play games of "Squash." But fair is fair, as per the old metaphor, "Why don't you pick on somebody your own size?" Maybe the dolphins' fission fusion society (in which individuals come and go at will) also includes shifts of social responsibility, something like Bette had been interacting with Celine when Celine got into trouble and it was therefore Bette's responsibility to get Celine out of trouble. Maybe no such rules exist, but being older, Bette "simply" recognized the calf's dilemma and rushed over to shepherd the calf to safety.

The most perplexing angle was that *the calf's mother hunted nearby without helping* at all. Dolphin mothers on the "Enchanted River" are very opinionated about their calf's schoolmates, although their interference fades as the calf grows older. Moreover, the calf's mother Celeste is a great mother. For example, she has taken Celine away from many situations that she deems dangerous or ill-advised, including our boat on occasion. Her perplexing lack of response to this episode has to be noteworthy.

The mother dolphin's lack of response suggested that there was no dilemma or need for rescue in that the senior bulls were *not* pouncing too hard on her calf. Celine herself went back to them three times; she was old enough to know the difference between play and aggression. The senior bulls won the short scuffle easily; why say they were still tense?

At issue was that the big bulls' pounces seemed aggressive to *us*, but evidently not to the mother dolphin. This was another example of what neuroscientist John Lilly called the bottlenose dolphins' good-natured violence. It is this dimension, behavior that looks rough to us but not to the dolphins, and details obscured by water that makes it so hard to interpret bottlenose dolphin behavior accurately.

Finally, the mother dolphin did not see any need to intervene but, for some reason, teen Bette did. Why?

The perplexity melts away if we say that dolphins live in a world without walls and can use that to their advantage. If this was one of those moments, the mother dolphin fed nearby while her calf tumbled innocently amid Bette and the bulls putting on quite a show for each other.

***

I see the show as follows. When the bulls traded punches, the senior bulls muscled the junior bulls in a quick lesson of what we call *"And Don't You Forget It!"* behavior. These are benign tournaments that establish relative rank, rather than murderous attacks. The five junior bulls accepted the lesson of lower rank from the two senior bulls. Though it *was* 5 against 2, they prudently retreated to digest their new information about the strength and pugnacity of these particular senior bulls and, dolphin like, stayed on the sidelines to see what happened next.

With an audience, the show must go on. Tournaments can do double duty as displays. When the bulls traded punches, it is reasonable to assume that they were also *stylin'* for the ladies. Bette would be pregnant in nine months and may have already been at the time in the technically available stage (that is, already "dating and mating"). But even if she was just standing in the doorway of her future sex life, it is never too early to start one's courtship efforts in a long-lived species with strong social memories, extended courtships, and a flair for showmanship.

Bette demonstrated her willingness and her ability to rescue a calf on three separate occasions. No one knows if dolphins demonstrate good mothering skills for the benefit of other dolphins. But clear precedent has been set by bird courtship which contains many symbolic demonstrations of attractive parental skills, including hunting and willingness to feed the young. Consider Bette's potential spectators. Seven bulls might now think twice before manhandling any of her future calves.

The calf's mother would remember Bette's intervention on her calf's behalf. The calf Celine would as well.

Last but not least, Rick was among the imputed spectators. Given the time that Rick and Better spent together, our guess is that he was the most likely father of her baby born the next year. What better way to draw [his] attention than to manufacture the calf's dilemma where none existed and rush over dramatically to shepherd it to safety?

Consider Bette's unique reaction to Rick's subsequent courtship towards her, shown in the picture below: She nuzzles him and swims off with her tongue hanging out! I have made enough observations of Bette's shy coquettishness towards Rick to think dolphins often behave to draw another dolphin's attention, similar to the way people sometimes behave to draw a specific person's attention.

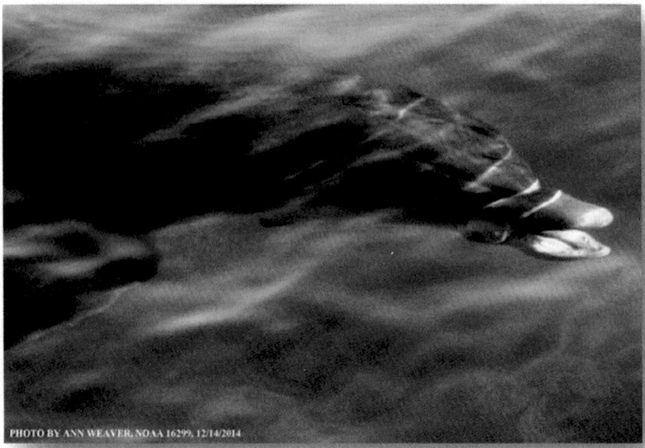

Bette Swims with her Tongue Hanging Out during her Courtship with Rick

***

When a dolphin rescues a calf, the gesture suggests that the rescuer recognizes that the calf does not recognize the risk – an example of bottlenose dolphins' ability to see another dolphin's viewpoint, a mental ability called perspective taking. The next story suggests another way that dolphins respond to another's perspective.

11. Sometimes You Need a Bigger Hammer

PHOTO BY ANN WEAVER, Ph.D., NOAA 16299, 5/4/2014

Specialized Dolphin Tailslap called a Kerplunk

***

How often are parents forced to adjust their tactics to persuade the child to obey?

There are times when a louder voice or microphone is needed to convey the message.

Echolocation, using sound waves instead of sight to scan their surroundings, is the dolphins' most unique physical capacity. The dolphins' second most unique physical capacity, the tailstock, could use some airtime. Fifty million years ago, early marine mammals (cetaceans) began the physical transformation that would eventually replace land legs with a sturdy tailstock. A tool of immense power and control, the tailstock is both a gas pedal and a steering wheel. It can propel its owner through water over twenty miles per hour and many feet into the air. It can be used to secure a holdfast with the seafloor or maintain position during aerial displays.

The tailstock can be used to tap the water surface daintily or slam it in anger. Its owner is capable of slugging it hard enough to break a man's neck yet soft enough to pet tenderly. Hard-hitting behaviors are called tailslaps.

Tailslaps come in many versions and have numerous uses. One version is specialized for hunting; the kerplunk, a two-pronged sound that the dolphin tail makes when smacked on the water surface in a way that shoots one wave backward and another upward in a water column up to ten feet high. Kerplunking is a hunting technique that is usually used to scare up something to eat, such as spooking fish out of hiding or into flight to make them easier to catch.

There is a special group of dolphins who occasionally visit our stretch of the "Enchanted River" where they use the kerplunking technique almost exclusively. They clearly coordinate with each other, more like their relatives the killer whales than local bottlenose dolphins.

In contrast, only a small percentage of local dolphins use the kerplunking technique and only on occasion. I think local dolphins know how to do it. They just do it occasionally, the way, for example, Americans use chopsticks occasionally. During their fleeting demonstrations, I also developed the impression that local dolphins might coordinate their kerplunks, rather like cymbal players who hit their cymbals alternately, not to hunt but to make some kind of social comment. It was hard to verify my impression that dolphins kerplunk socially when not hunting – until the winter day that verified that impression and gave me a striking new angle to consider.

Sybil, her six-month-old son Saga, and Saga's jolly male playmate Scrapefin Sam headed north. The baby and the bull play-wrestled heartily as they went, arching and rolling like playful puppies for half a mile. Sybil obviously trusted Sam and may have even been happy to have a babysitter. Saga was a wild child whom Sybil had disciplined repeatedly in the past, mainly because he would not stop playing and swim quietly at her side. In any case, she did nothing to interfere with their play.

They ducked into a cozy cove. Several dolphins were already hunting there, widely scattered and flushing out their fish food with kerplunks. Thus, the cozy cove was periodically pocked with water geysers that shot vertically six to eight feet into the air.

Usually, new dolphins seamlessly join dolphins who are already hunting. So there was no obvious reason why the incoming trio needed to gain acceptance from the dolphins already kerplunking in the cove. Yet, in an unparalleled gesture, Sybil and Sam entered the cove with an alternating series of synchronized kerplunks. Sybil kerplunked first. Sam gave an answering kerplunk. They ultimately gave several carefully synchronized kerplunks in turn, as if saying to the hunting dolphins that kerplunking was fine with them.

The other dolphins were too far away for us to say if they gave any response. They continued kerplunking in the distance. We settled in to see what happened next, expecting Sybil and Sam to scatter and hunt leaving young Saga to prance around amusing himself until they finished.

Instead, Sybil's son Saga and Scrapefin Sam resumed playing. It is hard to watch anything else when dolphins play. I am struck by the playful nature of mature bottlenose bulls on the "Enchanted River." I marvel at the amount of time they devote to play because among naturally occurring mammals kids play but adults usually do not, with the exception of dogs and cats.

The point is, we were riveted on the playing bull and calf. Sam would spring over and plunge young Saga into the brine. Saga would spring away in a half bid to be chased and bounce right back to his big playmate. Sam caught a fish here and there, giving Saga a few lessons in how this works. They dashed about, their pumping tails creating small hurricanes of tan mud in the green waters.

This entire time, Scrapefin Sam and Saga had been playing together while Sybil merely meandered nearby. I guess it was time for a change because Sybil decided to express herself with a striking combination of great showmanship and indirect tact.

Edging over to the cavorting males, Sybil began to systematically strike the water with her tailstock with rhythmic kerplunks like the stiff-legged march of soldiers.

Ker-PLUNK! Ker-PLUNK! Ker-PLUNK! We turned to her, riveted. Ker-PLUNK! Ker-PLUNK! Ker-PLUNK! She slugged her tail to a beat. Ker-PLUNK! Ker-PLUNK! Ker-PLUNK!

Sybil Puts on a Striking Display of 35 Specialized Tailslaps called Kerplunks

***

All told, Sybil carved out a frothy circle by kerplunking a record-breaking 35 times in a row!

Seeming oblivious to her striking gestures, the baby and bull kept playing. Edging closer to them, much to my amazement, Sybil whacked out seven more kerplunks. This was her way of signaling her calf Saga to return to her side.

Saga sidled to his mother's side and the two left the cove. Scrapefin Sam trailed them slowly.

This unmatched display of kerplunking had nothing to do with feeding. It remains unparalleled as an attention-getting gesture. So they *can* use kerplunks to make a social statement!

***

Oddly, that same month, we had two other demonstrations which showed that local dolphins use kerplunks to make social statements. Sybil's record-breaking demonstration seemed intended for her son. Another was intended for us and shows how far some wild dolphins will go to communicate. This brief moment need not have happened at all, except Bette decided it would.

During one dark January day on the second half of the survey, Captain John and I were cruising south along the "Enchanted River." Other than a single splash-and-dash dolphin that vanished before we could identify it, the survey had yielded nothing beyond a subdued sky of pastel and charcoal grays. Looking eternally upward, a pewter sea reflected the sky perfectly. Its dark calm rendered the usually-cheerful greens of the mangroves a deep fir color, as in the North Woods. Seaside homes shimmered vaguely in the distance. We were the only boat on the water. It was hushed, the only sound our research boat *Ms. Behavin's* purring engine. Visibility was perfect. Our view was a seamless steely monochrome in all directions, save for faint ripples from surprised sea creatures fluttering from the surface to the safety of the depths as we passed.

Thus, neither of us was prepared when a slim adult dolphin suddenly leapt right across our bow. It had to have traveled a considerable distance underwater to accomplish its sudden appearance. It was Bette. We plowed to a stop, pleasantly surprised that she had announced her presence so obviously. For the previous two years she had been unapproachable, following the sudden disappearance of her little daughter Ballou.

Bette came right over. She further punctuated her sudden presence with a leisurely slide under our bow. Surfacing nearby, she did three lazy kerplunks. Bette surfaced ten feet away and gave another lazy kerplunk. When she submerged, we settled in to watch this fantastic feeding technique.

But she never surfaced again! She utterly vanished. We had been ditched!

Why bother to make a showy entrance, only to leave abruptly? Her message: She was just swinging by to greet the boat but was otherwise busy.

*****

12. Dressing Up For a Dark Party

Dressing Up for Each Other - Reciprocal Self-Decoration!
Faye wears a wad of grass on her dorsal fin in the big picture.
Inset: Drake wears a caramel-colored coil (the egg case of a whelk) on his dorsal fin. Drake dressed up first and approached Faye.
Her response was to dress up too.

***

Between clothes, hats, shoes, and cologne, we all endeavor to put on a personality that defines us and makes us attractive to others. Are we the only ones?

A dozen dolphins streamed out from the oak-studded coastline and began writhing around our boat like people who had seen a ghost or were covered with ants. Pitching and rolling and spinning, the dolphins were clearly *very* excited, but in a good or bad way I could not - dared not - say.

All combinations of the highly-charged dolphins spun around each other in great excitement. Drake tried to mount our favorite flirt Celeste, who slid repeatedly out of reach. The arrival of two senior bulls precipitated a quick reassuring exchange between smaller bulls. Flanked by the senior bulls, a heavily pregnant female meandered around. A calf darted through the writhing wad; when it surged to the surface side by side with Faye, I snapped their picture and assumed it was her young son Falco. That picture would be priceless.

The dolphins split into two groups. One group left, leaving Faye alone with five very excited bulls of the Bowery Boys super-alliance (Drake, Reggie, Rick, Scrapefin Sam, and Ski). Faye mated them all wildly, almost as fast as she could.

Sex at sea is often hard to see. But there was no question about it today! I knew dolphins had recreational sex but this was super-charged! Electrified! I had never seen such uninhibited dolphin hubbub as this.

Many other behaviors were strange too.

Faye was a mom. Her little boy was a yearling called Falco after Jacques Cousteau's daring assistant. Dolphin moms with yearling calves are focused mothers and never, to my knowledge, the hub of unbridled sex like this.

But where was young Falco? The wild writhing hid his absence until the dolphins split into two groups. Falco was too young to have left with the departing group. He was too young to be out of sight. Just three weeks before, he had a wonderful morning of pleasant play with big bull Drake while his mom hunted nearby. This was normal for calves his age. In addition, Drake accompanied Faye so often that we thought they had a notably close relationship. In human terms, Drake was a dear friend of the family.

Drake was not part of the unbridled sex. He swam back and forth on the periphery of the action. He did nothing obvious to challenge the other bulls who were alternately and enthusiastically partnering with a very willing, almost desperate Faye. Why would a normal male of any species behave like that? Was it because his bonded bull buddy Bruce was not there to help him? I doubt it, because Drake had a plan: He *dressed up*...

I happened to be watching him as he swam thirty or so feet away from the excitement, ducked into the sea, and surfaced wearing a caramel-colored coil on his dorsal fin. It was an old egg case from marine snails known as whelks.

He swam directly to our boat, slid alongside it, and dropped his coil where I stood. I could have leaned over and grabbed it but was too startled by his stunning gesture to do it.

PHOTO BY ANN WEAVER, Ph.D., NOAA 16299, 4/23/2011

Drake Shows Me his Decoration

***

The egg case started to sink. Drake spun around, scooped it back onto his fin again, and swam directly over to Faye.

Her astonishing response was to dress up too. She immediately ducked into the sea and surfaced ablaze with emerald seagrass festooning her dorsal fin, shown in the opening picture with this story.

The two garlanded friends vanished together below the waves, taking the secret of “what happened next” with them.

***

I had seen dolphins wearing grass before this. But Faye showed that wearing grass is sometimes deliberate. I studied every grass-wearing episode closely and published my findings.[iii]

Based on data, self-decoration at sea has staggering implications: Dolphins dress up to attract attention. What person has NOT dressed up for the same reason?

The majority of resident dolphins have been seen dressing up with grass. This startling custom along the "Enchanted River" is an amazing demonstration of how local dolphins pay attention to what others are doing and are attracted to novelty - two very human behaviors.

***

But where was Faye's young son Falco? Back at the lab, I scrutinized the single photo of Faye and "her calf" I had taken in the field. The calf was not Falco.

It could take years to know if Drake and Faye dressed up because this is standard behavior on the "Enchanted River" or they were provoked by current circumstances.

I say this because we found Falco the next day - after a shark went for his jugular.

PHOTO BY ANN WEAVER, NOAA 16299, 4/24/2011

Grim Evidence of Young Falco's Fate

***

Little fated Falco's body floated belly-up, revealing that his throat had been ripped out by a shark. Before we condemn Mack the Knife for yet another crime, this is only circumstantial evidence. Did a shark kill little fated Falco? Or did he die of something else first and then the shark bit out his throat? We will never know.

***

An eerie piece of this gripping puzzle was unscientific kismet: Grass-wearing is the subject of local legend. These events happened in April. The February before, I received an email from someone who reads my newspaper column Dolphin Watch.[iv] "Have you ever heard what the old timers say about why dolphins wear grass?" she asked in her email. "They say dolphins wear grass to a funeral."

***

Dolphins on the "Enchanted River" tend to race around wildly under two circumstances: the right floes of food or big bad bull fights. Food attracts everybody within earshot. Fights attract dozens of dolphin on-lookers, propelled into wild sprints around the fighters. When wild racing is not clearly about food or fights, we are tempted to attribute it to the stimulating nature of a dolphin gathering itself. This story suggests that wild racing may sometimes result from a terrible discovery.

Animal behaviorists trained in science are discouraged from attributing emotions to the animals they study, and I have stated flatly in TV interviews that identifying dolphin emotions is extremely thorny.[v] Yet while the highly-charged atmosphere of this particular gathering was undeniable, I could not label it as happy excitement or serious distress at the time.

***

Faye's response in the wake of her son's death was unlike Sybil's response when her newborn died. People who experience the loss of a loved one deal with it as best we can. Such is life as we know it and perhaps life at sea as well.

True understanding of another species requires years of relationship building so that the presence of observers does not inhibit rare but significant events, like those of this dark but amazing morning. Otherwise, rare but significant events might never be seen.

***

Drake brought his caramel-colored egg case to our boat to *show* it to me. What kind of being behaves like that? The whelk egg case is made up of hundreds of individual nurseries, each the size of silver dollars, containing whelks the size of sesame seeds. Fresh egg cases are bright yellow (see the picture with story #25).

***

Faye in this story was the "first responder" in story #6, but not the day Saga danced with the devil. Why not? Three years before his devilish dance, in 2013, Faye and her next calf Facet died together. Instead of the grisly details, suffice it to say only that, as with humans, first responders often pay the ultimate price.

***

Wearing grass and egg cases have to be the dolphin's choice, because otherwise they work hard to remove anything on their bodies, as the next story shows.

*****

13. The Princess and the Pea

PeeWee Twists Helplessly as her Hitchhiking Remora moves Ticklishly Close to the Responsive Regions South of the Belly Button

***

The torment of a pebble in your shoe or an eyelash in your eye can drive you crazy. It seems that dolphins can suffer the same type of torment.

Cruising along the "Enchanted River" one warm spring day, we spied a small body in the distance shooting out of the water like a rocket, twisting in space wildly, and dropping onto the water in a big booming belly flop.

The distant dolphin rose and belly-flopped a second, third, fourth, and then fifth time. Today's little bucking bronco was a toddler called PeeWee, just nine months old. She began a new round of breaches under gossamer skies, which revealed an offending remora suctioned onto her baby belly.

Remoras do important work as cleaner fish. We do not know if they hurt, tickle, or just antagonize the exquisitely sensitive dolphin skin. But they drive dolphins wild!! If some creature crawled all over us like this, we would be wiggling too!

I started counting little PeeWee's breaches. As we watched her breach for the 17th time, Captain John recalled the fairy tale about the princess and the pea. In that story, a real princess is so delicate and sensitive that something as small as a pea disrupts her sleep.

Though this episode involved neither pea nor princess, the remora certainly disrupted poor little PeeWee. She breached continuously for the next twenty minutes. This was a long "remora rant" even for the energy of youth. After all, dolphins tire too. It takes energy to launch completely out of the water just once, much less dozens of times as PeeWee was doing.

Dolphin calves of the "Enchanted River" are plagued by remoras more than any other age class, maybe because they are growing and shed skin at appetizingly high rates. Calves are also plagued by remoras until they learn how to remove them.

While PeeWee breached and breached, her mom hunted nearby. Her mother, Priscilla, is a dolphin who conducts her affairs with a certain maritime majesty. She is picky about her companions, holds her own against other dolphins, once followed us to our local waterside McDonald's restaurant the time we changed our routine, uses us as babysitters by dropping her calves off at our boat, and even appears to use aerial behaviors to keep our attention. For these and other reasons, we call her *Queen* Priscilla.

As if unaware of PeeWee's maritime trampoline act, Queen Priscilla slowly searched a narrow cove lined with seaside homes. She snacked her way along, periodically circling around a fish, flinging it into the air, and lunging to grab and pop it down her throat.

PeeWee's breaching display drew onlookers from seaside homes who gathered along the shoreline to watch, clapping and laughing as if the little dolphin was performing for them.

PeeWee Leaps to Remove her Belly-riding Hitchhiker Remora

***

Someone shouted, “Who is it? What’s going on?”

“Peewee has a remora!” I shouted back through cupped hands. “She’s trying to tear it off!”

“Oh! Poor little Peewee!”

When PeeWee had breached over forty times in a row, I started to see her behavior differently. Was this tickling or torment? Filming PeeWee’s suffering, was I guilty of being a shameless member of the paparazzi?

If dolphins are so smart, why didn’t Priscilla just yank the annoying remora off? Why didn’t she show PeeWee how to shave it off by sliding along the sea floor? To do that, Priscilla needed to understand Peewee’s situation. In other words, she needed to have a *theory of mind*, which is taking someone else’s perspective. Humans do this constantly.

Questions of if and how dolphins take someone else’s perspective have yet to be met with firm evidence. Nonetheless, bottlenose dolphins behave in several ways that suggest they are aware of other dolphins’ situation – that is, have some theory of mind. They babysit. They intervene for other dolphins’ calves. They help dolphins who are hurt or stressed. They have helped *people* who are hurt or stressed. They even *share fish with human fishermen* in some parts of the world.

By now, PeeWee had breached over sixty times! Priscilla had to understand that PeeWee was highly excited about something; dolphins rarely leap like *this*. Even if Priscilla understood that PeeWee was trying to remove the remora, she did not appear to see remora removal as her job.

Intriguingly, PeeWee breached closer and closer to her mother. Leaping dolphins can misjudge where they land. But they don't do it often. They typically aim their landings specifically, usually careful to avoid other dolphins but sometimes landing next to one in threat or landing on another dolphin in anger. Once the number of Peewee's breaches hit eighty-something, she was landing next to her mother, sending big booming waves over her.

Was Peewee throwing a tantrum? Elephant biologists Ian and Oria Douglas-Hamilton wrote in their narrative *Among the Elephants* about the time they watched an elephant throw a 'first-rate tantrum' while the rest of her herd browsed placidly nearby.

Priscilla responded to PeeWee's big booming belly flops by swimming away - all the way down to the end of a narrow cove where she caught a fish, turned around, and slowly returned to PeeWee. PeeWee stayed at her side after that, reduced to occasional body shudders still trying to remove the remora. The clapping crowd along the shoreline disbanded. Priscilla and Peewee joined bull Scrapefin Sam and female Sabine in the next bay. Life resumed its rhythm.

Did Peewee breach 100 times in a row because she was being tickled, tormented, or throwing a tantrum? When and how she rid herself of the remora also remains a mystery: Dolphin field work keeps many secrets.

***

Priscilla did nothing obvious to help PeeWee remove the remora. One possibility is that Priscilla had no clue about PeeWee's dilemma. Another is that Priscilla was aware of PeeWee's dilemma, given dolphins' close observation of each other, but did not see it as her problem to solve. Priscilla's behavior is the common response among dolphin moms whose calves have remoras: They do nothing about it. This highlights the few mothers who try to bite the remora off their bucking calves, including Bette and Lana.

***

Dolphins of the "Enchanted River" jump out of the water for many different reasons – many of which are unfathomable. An obvious reason is ridding themselves of remoras. This relates to the fact that dolphins reject anything touching their skin that they did not put there themselves.

The idea that PeeWee started her 100 breaches by trying to remove the remora but ended them as a tantrum next to her mother is an intriguing possibility. Like human toddlers, ape and monkey kids from gorillas to capuchins throw temper tantrums when their desires are thwarted. So do elephants. I have also seen two different adult dolphins breach about 20 times each, though neither had a remora.

PeeWee's 100-breach display was the only episode that suggested a tantrum, but I submit that still does not justify calling Queen Priscilla's daughter a princess!

***

PHOTO BY ANN WEAVER, Ph.D., NOAA 1088-1815, 9/25/2010

PeeWee Demonstrates her Remora Removing Skills

***

A year and a half later, PeeWee demonstrated that she had learned to remove remoras with two good body smacks.

Before we end her story, I included a picture of another time PeeWee was carried away, this time literally. PeeWee balanced on the back of a smaller playmate as the latter swam along, a tricky backward “piggy back” maneuver that takes cooperation and coordination.

PeeWee is Taken for an Unusual Ride

*****

*** *Behavior toward the Boat* ***

14. Our Favorite Flirt

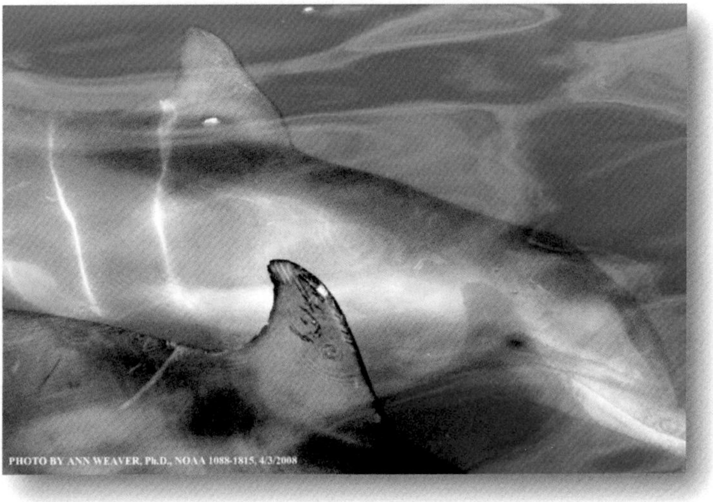

PHOTO BY ANN WEAVER, Ph.D., NOAA 1088-1815, 4/3/2008

Our Favorite Flirt Celeste Herds a Calf Away from our Boat

***

As we go about our daily business, we may need to modify our actions to deal with those who are uncomfortable with us. Otherwise, someone could yell at us without warning.

A cute baby dolphin wiggled over to our boat and flitted around it like a butterfly. It was already a beautiful day at sea, but the baby made it perfect. As I watched and recorded it, time slowed to the rhythm of the sea and immersed me in its embrace.

An adult dolphin materialized next to the boat, snorted out a coarse cough vocalization, and swiftly ushered the calf away from that *creepy* boat.

A wild dolphin had just yelled at us!

The snorting dolphin was a local lady we call Celeste. The calf she ushered away was not hers, which apparently didn't matter. It must have been the principle of the thing.

Protective behavior like this, but mainly melting away, happened until Celeste became used to our presence – became habituated to us – which took two years.

When she finally habituated, it was as abrupt as flipping a switch. One day, she was melting away as usual. The next day she let us watch, and has continued to do so. Either she understood that we meant no harm or resigned herself to this annoying boat buzzing around her at intervals. The suddenness of dolphin acceptance still surprises me; the months or years required to acclimate wild dolphins to close observation does not.[vi]

Once Celeste became habituated, we could draw near without changing her behavior. Becoming part of her background was a precious turning point for me. I want to understand dolphins on their own terms - without disturbing them.

But the truth is, accepting us *did* change Celeste's behavior. She became a frustrating flirt!

For instance, Celeste sometimes acts like a professor who would come to my university office and pry open a conversation when I was clearly busy. Once I stopped what I was doing and was mid-sentence in reply, she would spin and march away. I never understood whether I was supposed to follow her. Similarly, Celeste catches our attention by swinging by the boat at close range. But unlike the chatty professor, we *will* follow the dolphin and Celeste knows it. Here are some ways she uses that knowledge.

Celeste gets us driving in circles. She and her calf Celine swim ahead of us steadily a distance of 60-80 feet (3-4 boat lengths or 18-24 m). We follow. They submerge and stop. We do not know they stopped and keep going, so we overshoot them. They surface behind us 3-4 boat lengths away. We obediently turn around and go back. Again unbeknownst to us, they glide the opposite way underwater. They appear the same distance away *behind us again*, surfacing where we turned around!

Humans tire of this game before dolphins do.

Celeste sometimes leads us to other dolphins. One summer day, while we were near the little beach where dogs and their owners run free, two dolphins flashed by the boat like a single flicker of a match in the dark. Celeste and her calf Celine surfaced several boat lengths ahead of us, moving at speed. Each time we lost sight of them and slowed, uncertain of their path, they also seemed to slow and then sped up after we resighted and resumed following them. They led us to a hidden group. Compliments of Celeste, we spent the next half hour delightedly surrounded by a dozen dozing dolphins. Celeste, by the way, did not stay.

Celeste sometimes acts out the idea of not wanting something until somebody else has it. She and her calf Celine will be too busy hunting in one area to have their pictures taken. Yet if we go to the next group of dolphins to take their pictures, lo and behold, there is Celeste among them!

Celeste may have also once used the boat to escape bothersome bulls. She and Celine swam with a long-term female skeptic and two unhabituated bulls. Skeptics and unhabituated dolphins do not "do boats." The bulls were putting the moves on Celeste, but when she began swimming close to our boat, they backed off, very upset.

One bull shot out of the water, breaching wildly in the distance with his mouth wide open and slamming down like a falling tree. Dolphins often breach like this when they are upset with others, like a person thumping the table instead of the person who upset them.

The other bull ripped up the seafloor, creating a massive cloud of mud in the water we call a mud plume. Dolphins often make mud plumes like this when they are upset with others. The bulls approached the girls no more, though they trailed them for the next hour.

These observations are remarkable *because* Celeste switched from skeptic to flirt. Moreover, the year she accepted our presence, we saw her more often per survey than any other dolphin. When we see a dolphin more than once per survey, we call subsequent sightings "resights." It is possible to resight a dolphin because our surveys are systematic in that we cover the same waters the same way every time. As predictably as possible, we go north a specific distance, turn around at the same spot, go south a specific distance, and go back to the same dock we left from.

Like a school bus that stops at all railroad crossings, we stop at all dolphins. We might see Celeste in the morning to the north with one set of dolphins and later that day to the south with different dolphins. This was presumably her natural schedule.

Or was it? When we resighted Celeste two, three, or four times *per survey* that year, was she really just going about her business? How many times did we have to repeatedly resight her during a survey before we reject the idea that her swimming schedule matched our survey route accidentally?

These observations beg the question of how much Celeste knows about our routine at sea. If she thinks about it at all, she undoubtedly knows more about our predictable same-time-every-time (systematic) routine than we know about hers. Equipped as she is with superb sound tracking abilities, she can *also* track us by our vocalizations – our monotone outboard engine.

Celeste recognized our interest in her. Maybe, for a short time this sparked a reciprocal interest in us - a glimpse of bottlenose dolphin psychology. As a thinking animal, does Celeste ever *test us* like some maritime experimental psychologist? Say, who studies who out there?

*****

15. Mystery at McDonald's

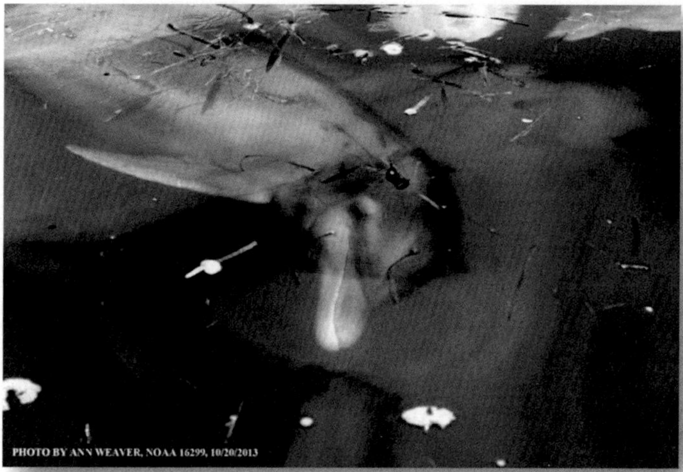

PHOTO BY ANN WEAVER, NOAA 16299, 10/20/2013

Priscilla Studies Us as We Study Her at McDonald's

***

Have you ever watched somebody when they did not know you were watching them? How did you keep them from noticing your gaze?

Watching someone who does not realize they are being watched can be very informative. Too bad we can never sneak up on the dolphins we study and watch them unawares, because Captain John and I trail them in our small research boat, *Ms Behavin'*. Just as their excellent hearing abilities enable them to distinguish their voices among themselves, it is likely that they identify us by our boat's hull and engine sound profile. Moreover, they probably hear us coming for miles.

The dolphins are obviously aware of us. But they rarely make this obvious. As time went on and we came to know each other, we built a mutual trust. Now they often come over to the boat in greeting and return to the business at hand, which is perfect for our work.

However, one day we changed our survey routine, and the dolphins did not return to the business at hand.

It was a late winter day. The winds were high. The seas were cold and messy. Even the "Enchanted River" was punchy with swells and toppling breakers. By this point, we had surveyed it 150 times. So when we found two mother-calf pairs plowing through the sloppy seas, Sybil and her son Steve with Queen Priscilla and her son Puck, we knew them and they presumably knew us. But *how well* they knew us came into question.

Our boat *Ms. Behavin'* pitched and yawed drunkenly. I braced to take data and pointlessly tried to protect my camera against countless sprays of saltwater.

Sybil Arching to Breathe in Sloppy Seas

***

The cresting waves of heavy seas force dolphins to raise their heads higher than normal over the water surface to breathe without taking in water. This extra effort is tiring, just as swimming in heavy seas is tiring, for even physically fit humans. Toddlers in their first winter, Steve and Puck lunged and pounced at the surface to breathe. Today their struggle for existence was visible.

When the dolphins arched their heads higher than normal to breathe, they seemed to glance at us over the toppling froth. These little "sneak-a-peeks," which they used to look above the water, were flattering. Then I reminded myself that the dolphins' glances were just related to trying to breathe in heavy seas. Later I would wonder.

Some dolphin surveys of the "Enchanted River" are Heaven on earth. This one was the opposite. We were tossed like ping pong balls in seething seas. We were sticky from endless showers of salt spray. It was cold. Tumbling toward a seaside McDonald's restaurant some time later, we decided to stop for reinforcements. It was the first time we had done this on a survey. It felt guilty. John went in. Because the restaurant was crowded, it took him awhile to return with nice steaming coffee.

As we prepared to launch, Sybil and Steve suddenly surfaced beside the boat in a little sneak-a-peek and then vanished!

Had they followed us to McDonald's? We laughed and said they followed us for the 2-for-1 "Filet of Fish Sandwich Meal Deal," then wondered what this was about. There wasn't a simple explanation. It had been half an hour since we left the dolphins behind so they had not simply followed our wake. The engine was off so they had not simply followed our sound trail. They could have been going this way anyway. But they still had to come all the way to the restaurant's dock at the back of the little cove. Finally, they never have to surface beside the boat, unless they needed a good look to make sure it was really us - if that's what they were doing.

On our next survey, we were watching bulls Drake and Ski when they suddenly sprinted towards distant dolphins, who turned out to be Queen Priscilla and her toddler son Puck. The calf played as the adults hunted nearby. Data collected, it was time to move on.

Nearing McDonald's, we took the opportunity to do a field experiment. Out of our ordinary routine, I proposed, "Let's stop for coffee again and see what happens," never dreaming anything would. It was the second time we stopped for coffee on a dolphin survey. It still felt guilty.

As I returned with the coffee, Priscilla and Puck surfaced with a frank sneak-a-peek near the boat! Nearby, Drake tossed a fish and lunged at the gull that pounced to steal it.

I remind myself that my interest in the dolphins does not mean that the dolphins are interested in me. But as my Dad, skeptic and surely no animal lover, once asked, "Why can't they be as curious about you as you are about them?"

*****

16. The Accidental Easter Bonnet

PHOTO BY ANN WEAVER, Ph.D., NOAA 1088-1815, 4/5/2007

Bette Leaps in Greeting

***

We become familiar with the appearance of people we see on a regular basis. When they occasionally change their appearance, how long does it take to adjust to their new look?

One tender spring morning I found myself humming Irving Berlin's famous song, "I could write a sonnet, about your Easter bonnet, and of the girl I'm taking to the Easter parade." In the spirit of the season, I switched my usual visor to a new "Easter bonnet" visor to wear at sea.

It never occurred to me to ask if the dolphins would still recognize me if I wore a different hat.

A dolphin swimming around at sea has several ways to recognize our research boat *Ms. Behavin'*. As an expert in vibrational language, it could identify us by the sound of our boat's particular combination of outboard engine and hull design, and the familiar way the combination made its body resonate.

It could also recognize us by a pair of plastic flukes attached to the stem of our outboard engine that are almost identical in appearance to dolphin flukes. They are useful for keeping the boat level in the water at speed, but few boats in our area have them.

The dolphin could also recognize the big black shapes against the white sides of our boat. It would not know that the black shapes spell RESEARCH. But its dolphin eyes have decent vision in the air and easily recognize patterns with striking contrasts like black against white.

Finally, it could recognize our silhouettes from its vantage at the water surface, although looking up at the sky makes its squint. It could note that Captain John's silhouette does not change much: He is an upright human who stands in one spot, at the helm, steering. It could note that I change the boat's silhouette by bouncing back and forth between the computer station and forward deck where I stand to take pictures. It might also note that I am the one with the weird human silhouette from a terrible growth on the right side of my face - my beloved camera and long lens.

To any dolphin squinting at my silhouette, the camera is a constant but hats change it. I wore a visor for years (no change). Then I switched to baseball caps. When I did, we thought we noticed vague changes in the dolphins' behavior. But coming closer or glancing at us "more than usual" did not convince me that they noticed I wore a different hat. Captain John, however, remains convinced that they did.

Ann's Seaside Silhouette

***

Then came winter. My silhouette changed again. I started wearing a knit wool ski cap bought in the mountains of Utah. It is snugly warm and to my mind the dumbest-looking cap I have ever worn. Its cone-head silhouette and yarn tassel looks hip on 15-year-old snowboarders with open jackets and bright red cheeks. Me? I look idiotic. But I am warm.

When my cone-head silhouette first appeared on the bow, we again thought we noticed unusual dolphin behavior but again weren't sure. Were the dolphins really coming closer than usual and/or glancing up more often?

That spring, I changed hats again. This time, I wore a sun-repellant canvas safari hat that covers as much head, face, and shoulders as possible without being a hood with eye slits. The first day I wore my strikingly different "accidental Easter bonnet," the dolphins' behavior was strikingly different too. Every dolphin that day came over. Some circled the boat slowly at close range.

All did the rare but conspicuous behavior we call *snorting the engine*. Dolphins "snort the engine" by directly aiming their faces at the stem and flukes of the outboard engine, which is always out of gear when dolphins are near to avoid mutilating them with a spinning propeller. They presumably "snort" to read the vibrations closely, echolocate for specific details, or both.

They don't snort the engine often. But the day of my "accidental Easter bonnet" canvas safari hat, they all did. Were they double-checking our identity, having recognized us "as usual" (whatever that means) but confused by my new hat?

***

Consider our big-brained cousins, the pygmy chimps or bonobos. My bonobo buddy Lana lived at the San Diego Zoo. Regardless of how many months I'd been away or what I was wearing, she could pick me out of a *sea* of zoo visitors and would race over to the window of her enclosure to greet me as excitedly as did my human friends.

The fact that I wore different clothes made her long-term memory of me even more impressive because apes never change clothes. As such, we would not expect them to have the mental ability to understand that: "The clothes change but the individual stays the same." When Lana made this mental leap, she generalized. She showed inductive reasoning. That is, she drew a general conclusion (recognizing me) from individual observations (my different outfits).

Dolphins never change clothes either. But their complicated social lives are possible because of their excellent long-term memories. They recognize dolphins they have not seen in years. In addition, we know from captive studies that dolphins excel at generalizing (inductive reasoning).

In a third scenario, consider my parrot Rita. I raised her from a naked nestling and she is imprinted on me. Nonetheless, if I approach her wearing a towel turban after washing my hair, she recoils in terror. The turban obliterates my identity for her. She apparently does not recognize me by my voice, which I find strange given that birds are sound-based animals. She is unable to draw on 25 years of experience that my clothes change but I stay the same. She does not mentally deduce that the turbaned woman who sounds and acts like me actually IS me. I cannot pick her up until I remove the turban without risking painful repercussions.

***

Observations like the day of my “accidental Easter bonnet” suggest that the dolphins differentiate between the boat and the people in it. How do they recognize people? How important are silhouettes?

The incidents of the “accidental Easter bonnet” also suggest that wild dolphins may double-check secondary sources of information, such as snorting the engine, to verify its signature features. It is also very possible they were checking for other changes that we do not sense.

On the other hand, maybe it was all a dream, like the Easter bunny, or that my canvas safari hat remotely resembled an Easter bonnet, even an accidental one!

*****

17. How a Dolphin Might Launch a Conversation

Welles Prepares to Toss a Fish

***

Experts say, "Start a conversation by asking about the other person's interests." That is impossible with those at sea. What are the alternatives?

The hardest dolphins to study at sea are the bulls. They do not appear to be curious about the boat, show no interest in playing with it, and go about their business at sea with directness and without distraction. However, most of them eventually habituate to our presence and let us glimpse their watery world.

One pair of bonded bulls, Orson and Welles, took their time to habituate to us - although I am not sure if it was the closeness of our boat or our blunt interest in their activities to which they objected for so long.

Both bulls are big and memorable. Orson is memorable like a prize fighter who took too many punches in the face. In fact, the first word I said when I saw his mauled dorsal fin was, *"Ouch!"* Some long-ago shark encounter left a necklace of small scars from sharp teeth on both sides of his fin, and may also be responsible for its broad strip that undergoes curious color changes from time to time. His fin also has three big "keyhole" or round notches, probably from other bulls biting him. Orson is a memorable mug.

His buddy Welles is no "pretty boy" either but has fewer scars. He is especially memorable for the bright mid-summer's day he decided to have a go at us.

Orson and Welles were in the middle of a long courtship with Queen Priscilla. Her daughter Paisley was three years old. So mom was probably dating again. However, as we have learned, there is no sense rushing anything on the "Enchanted River," especially romance. Local courtships can last for months… which is plenty of time to think of ways to keep life interesting (like the captive orangutan in story #1).

Orson, Welles, Priscilla, and young miss Paisley were scattered across a cozy cove at the end of our study area. Its entrance along the "Enchanted River" is narrow and easily missed. Yet this charming cove has evidently been popular with local fisherman for a long time because, as our sonar indicates, its seafloor is generously strewn with flotsam from ancient anchors to rusty crab traps. The dolphins were searching for snacks among the flotsam and were hard to see.

We finally spied Welles searching along a shoreline. We tracked him by the pulses of big bubbles he shot into the seas to scare fish into flight. He did not acknowledge our presence in any way.

After we hovered for a while, he slid over to a sandbar in the middle of the cove where the water is hip deep. He submerged and created small mud plumes, which dolphins do regularly in the course of securing their prey. We glimpsed a bright flash in the dark green waters: Welles was swimming upside-down the way dolphins do when they are pursuing a fish at close range. The bright flash was his white belly briefly gleaming against jade waters.

Abruptly, the rounded head of this massive male bobbed out of a mud plume four or five times, barely clearing the water surface. Then he sunk vertically into the sea.

The waters began swaying and cresting as if he thrashed wildly underneath and unseen. Another massive mud plume arose. Welles bobbed again. But his head did not break the surface before it sank this time. He seemed to be straining against something.

On board we rippled with alarm. Was Welles tangled in something? God knows this was the cove for it. Creating swelling surges and the mud plumes, was he struggling mightily against a terrible snare as he strained to reach the air?

We quickly debated if this was the moment to dive in and save a dolphin from drowning. Could we? Should we?!

The muddy waters writhed but hid all. Like the dolphin thrashing in front of me, a thousand thoughts crashed through my mind: my morals, the hands-off policy of my federal permit, my ethics, the let-nature-take-its-course edict of field research, the madness of watching something die that we could save, the danger of trying to save it, the danger of dying by trying.

Time slowed for us on board, but not for the big bull thrashing below the surface.

***

When a person could hold their breath no longer, Welles erupted like a geyser. Crashing back down on the water surface, he slammed the seas and kicked a fish over our bow in a colossal column of water!

Welles surfaced seamlessly and headed for his distant schoolmates. As he left, he cast an unforgettable backward glance as if to say,"Did ya catch *THAT*?"

Our human interpretation of this event with Welles was completely off target. I wonder, Was that the idea?

Welles Casts an Unforgettable Parting Glance

18. The Dolphins and Dr. Dolittle

Mom and Son Surf the Same

***

We think we truly know somebody when we can anticipate their needs and actions by their behavior. Dr. Dolittle could do this with the animals, but he was a fictional character. What does a poor dolphin have to do to make humans understand it?

One gauzy December day, two dolphins passed a small green and beige island as they glided safely over its treacherous skirt of sharp oyster shells. Diana, the mother, was sleepy. Doodle, the son on whom she doted, pranced like a colt at her side. He was three years old and wide awake. The blue-green waters were starting to cool for the winter. Liking cool waters as dolphins do, Doodle wiggled as they went.

They heard a familiar sound in the distance. It was that boat that hangs around dolphins unless the dolphins ditch it. Boats can be useful. Slow boats are good for catching a nap. Fast boats are good for catching a ride.

As expected, that boat was heading over.

Reciprocating, mother and son headed towards our approaching boat. Once dolphins and boat converged, sleepy Diana settled on a pretty swimming pattern we call "crisscross travel." Side by side, mom and son surfaced on one side of the boat, slid invisibly underneath it, and surfaced on the other side of the boat, back and forth – crisscrossing us rhythmically in a tranquil waltz.

They crisscrossed for a while and drew ever closer until they were weaving just under the bow at the front of the boat. Their closeness pulled me. I leaned over the railing, hypnotized by their sleek flowing bodies. I thought I heard the distant siren's call...

No. That was a dolphin whistle. Snapping back to reality and seeing the dolphins weaving under the bow, I saw the pattern that dolphins everywhere use to say they would like to surf.

I called back to Captain John, "I think they want to surf."

Asking *us* to surf was an odd request. *Ms Behavin'* is a small worthy craft but not a good surfing boat because of her size and weight. I have also done my best to be a cardboard cut-out around all of the animals I have studied, NOT reacting, engaging, interacting, or interfering with them despite showing up - year after year – to study their behavior. For example, the apes and monkeys I have studied undoubtedly saw me as the most boring person they had ever met.

Well. It was almost Christmas. Once can't hurt. I gave in to temptation and nodded at John half-heartedly. He sped up, but uncertainly, because we don't play with the dolphins because science is serious and stolid, right? He didn't go too fast and the dolphins didn't surf. We circled back to them.

They resumed weaving back and forth under the front of the boat in the universal request to surf. Yet the boat still chugged along slowly. More drastic measures were required.

Diana suddenly startled like someone had goosed her from behind, and being directly overhead, leaning over the railing, I could see that no one had. She shot forward with a rapid and powerful downward swipe of her tailstock, her sudden forward lurch leaving an obvious trail of foam behind her.

"Hit it!" I cried to the captain. John gunned the engine. *Ms. Behavin'* roared into life!

And so did the dolphins! They shot into our wake, silver torpedoes glinting under translucent jade waves.

Diana had figured out how to ask those dull-witted humans if they could surf.

***

Captain John glanced back to see Doodle leap into the air and shouted, "Where have I seen that move before?" The first time was four years before when Diana used the very same move to surf when she was three weeks pregnant with Doodle.

***

Diana's decision to start the surfing by snapping her tailstock down was intriguing. The physical action of her "peduncle snap" is the same motion that Southern California dolphins, who are champion surfers, use to launch themselves into passing waves to surf them. It is also functionally comparable to the way human surfers, body surfers, and boogie boarders launch themselves into passing waves to surf them. The peduncle snap accomplishes a sudden burst of speed for the dolphins. But, could it also be another *symbol* of surfing, the way a person dips their head as a symbol of the respect shown by bowing and curtsying?

A dolphin trying to grab a person's attention has to make their move where the human will see it. So it was also intriguing that Diana did her peduncle snap at the front of our boat because this is the direction that most boaters face.

Finally, it was also intriguing that Diana, not her son Doodle, made the request to surf. She was sleepy when we found them and likewise surfed only briefly. It was Doodle who had the energy to surf and surf and surf. Did his mom ask for him?

***

People and dolphins love to surf. But those dramatic glides into shore on magnificent breakers crashing off Hawaii and California are only dreams on the west coast of Florida. Western Florida waves are tamed by the gentle slopes of the continental shelf long before they reach the shore, mostly gliding onto the beaches as small gentle folk that merely lick the sand and back humbly away. Our beaches are not designed for surfing. They are designed for mindfulness.

Nonetheless, some of the dolphins of the "Enchanted River" do surf artificial waves provided by boats. They surf for fun, which guarantees spine-tingling exhilaration for observers, and probably the dolphins too. They also surf for surprisingly practical reasons, using boats as taxis and get-away cars to move more easily up and down the waterways. Both fun and practical surfing styles mean learning to recognize the right boats and sometimes talking to the right boat captains.

***

I told a colleague of mine about Diana's request and commented that the dolphins probably think we are the stupidest humans they know. He stoutly disagreed, "They probably think you are the smartest!"

*****

19. Seaside Bait-and-Switch

PHOTO BY ANN WEAVER, Ph.D., NOAA 16299, 6/9/2013

PeeWee and Friend Go Surfing

***

April Fool's Day is a holiday reserved for playing tricks, so we stay alert for possible tricks all day. What about the rest of the year?

The bank that was going to give me my first home loan tried a bait-and-switch. The day of the signing, they produced a new, more expensive loan document and expected me to sign it. Today, most of us have seen some bait-and-switch naughtiness on land. Should we watch out for it at sea too?

Captain John and I were heading at speed along "The Raceway," the longest stretch of the study area between slow speed zones. If a boat captain is going to work up a good head of steam, this is the place. Boaters who speed up unzip the water in front of them and leave large waves behind them that nearby dolphins can surf if the boat design is right and the dolphin is so inclined.

We spied bulls Bruce and Drake up ahead and slowed down to approach them. They were taking a mobile catnap. They swam sleepily in perfect rhythm about five feet apart. Drake swung over to say hello and slid back to his buddy, seamlessly resuming the hypnotic cadence of their sleepy swimming.

By and by, a handsome yacht rolled past at speed. Suddenly awake, the bulls sprinted over and vanished into its wake. Captain John paced the yacht so that I could snap pictures to identify and document the surfing dolphins when they leapt out of their mobile water slide to breathe.

The dolphins surfed for a mile. John paced them perfectly, albeit at a distance - to keep our little research boat safely clear of that voluminous wake.

Later, back at the lab, my photo identification pictures were cheerfully vindicated when they revealed a seaside bait-and-switch! We saw Bruce and Drake vanish *into* the wake of the speeding yacht. But the pictures I took of the dolphins leaping out of the wake of the speeding yacht were of PeeWee and a friend! No sign of the big bulls!

Whether in our world or the dolphins' world, and whether by the magician's old sleight of hand or a modern bait-and-switch, we need to be aware that what we think we see may not be the case.

***

Dolphin photo identification takes fast reflexes, which are underscored by an unsuspected limitation of the human body. When watching a dolphin surface through my camera's viewfinder, I can either snap its picture or identify who it is. There is not enough time to do both. It only takes a split second to identify the dolphin. But that is still too late to trigger my finger to press the camera's button and snap the picture – even though it only takes a split second for a thought in my brain to turn into action in my finger.

It is this same fraction of a second that a professional baseball batter has to decide whether or not to swing at the ball.

20. Spooky Action at a Distance

Sabine Slides along her Mom Tenderly

***

Emotional connection with loved ones, even if separated by distances, is the basis of a functional society. It's a simple thread that ties us together. With easy access to world travel, we can enjoy the shared emotions of other cultures that were previously alien or isolated from us. This unexpected gift can cross many boundaries and makes us consider how, though different, we share a thread of understanding.

The warm summer's day that shed otherworldly light on this thread was nothing short of spooky.

Some kids never leave home, and Sabine was one of them. Sabine and her mother - whom we simply called Sabine's Mom - were very close. Sabine never showed the standard process of weaning, in which the growing calf stretches the attachment leash to its mom until it snaps and the teen dolphin leaves to live an independent life. In fact, Sabine never left her mother.

Her mother left her. One winter day, she disappeared. Her story just stopped - ending without an ending. We had no clue about her disappearance.

Sabine changed dramatically. She spent more time alone over the next two years than any other time that decade. Uncharacteristically, she often left when other dolphins approached. She stopped stopping by the boat. Previously a popular babysitter, she stopped playing with baby dolphins.

I cannot say that Sabine mourned her mother because her behavior change made sense for her age. Dolphins who are weaned of their mother's company and care, whether abruptly like Sabine or gradually like most, enter what we on the "Enchanted River" call the Phantom Phase. The cheerful bravery of the calf in its mother's care is replaced by vanishing acts. "Phantoms" are small and swift teens that see flash by the boat, leaving observers to wonder if they saw a dolphin at all. We find Phantoms hunting alone in hidden coves, feeding fanatically. In glaring contrast to their behavior as calves, they become hard to approach as teens. They eventually relinquish their solitary phase, becoming more social over time. Like our own teens on land, the time and intensity of the Phantom Phase varies at sea.

Still, Sabine had been so *obviously* affectionate with her mother that I cannot believe she did not mourn. Mourning is the process of reorganizing yourself - physically, mentally, and socially - when confronted with the awful absence of a companion around whom your life revolved. Mourning is a terribly permanent form of weaning.

Dolphins are emotional animals, all hidden by that eternal smile, and are extremely dependent on each other. Captive dolphins who lose a friend can become inconsolable. They do not eat. They do not perform. Sometimes, they do not recover. Sometimes, they recover slowly.

In any case, Sabine vanished into her Phantom Phase. As for me, I kept an eye out for Sabine's Mom.

Two years passed. Dolphins were fanned out over shallow waters in the shadow of a seaside hospital on the shores of the "Enchanted River." As I picked my way after them, I quite abruptly thought about Sabine's Mom.

It was a memory with teeth. The image of her dorsal fin, like a face to me, flashed onto the screen of my mind with dreamy clarity. As I tracked the dorsal fins ahead of me, I again wondered where she was (*if* she was) and how she was doing. It hurts, not knowing. So quietly, they crawl into one's heart.

My feelings about dolphins drive my efforts, of course. But they are separate from my work to understand them. I focus on what I can see. Yet, there in my mind's eye, I could not help but see Sabine's Mom. It was a quintessentially private moment when the field biologist confronts their feelings about a particular animal. Unbidden, my heart shot into the ethers. I gripped the steering wheel, bowed my head, squeezed my tearing eyes, and was flooded with profound emotion, "Oh, Sabine's Mom... Where *are* you? I *miss* you!"

A new emotion flooded me: Guilt. "Yeah. *I* miss Sabine's Mom. ***I*** miss Sabine's Mom? What about *Sabine*? Oh, *poor Sabine!*"

I suddenly felt sick for Sabine the way I felt sick when my dad died. I ached for her. I empathized with her. I saw her months of solitude; her hesitance with the boat; her slow return to a social life. Statistics and spreadsheets aside, Sabine would ultimately become a normal social creature with many companions and a full dolphin life once again. But those first months *must* have been tough for her.

The day became vivid, like I had never seen those familiar shallows or gray dolphin fins before. Never had I wanted so desperately to know what dolphins think and feel, and how much of our human experience accurately applies to them. If *only* I could know what happened to Sabine's Mom and come to some kind of closure.

For a scientist so rigorously trained to discount the emotional side of animal behavior, it was spooky. I was glad I was alone. None of my colleagues should see me act like this. Wild dolphins are not pets, and I was not supposed to *care* about them...

Lost in thought, or maybe out of habit, I glanced behind me. A lone dolphin was approaching. I clicked the throttle into neutral and floated, expecting it to cut past and join the others.

Instead, it came directly to the boat. The only wild dolphins who do this are the cursed creatures turned into beggars by thoughtless people who feed them.

Even more singular, it slid along the length of the boat the way dolphins slide along each other tenderly.

I could have leaned over and touched it.

It was Sabine.

I could have fallen out of the boat.

Sabine wove around the boat for a timeless time, as she had around her mom all those years past.

We had not seen Sabine among the other dolphins that day, that month, or that season.

Albert Einstein drew the line at something he called "spooky action at a distance." Officially, his spooky action is called "quantum entanglement." Theoretically, if two particles are vibrating in unison, they can retain their synchronization even if separated by profound distances because they are tied together with a thread of energy called a Schrödinger wave. Changes in one particle could be transmitted to the other particle instantly.

Like most of Einstein's other theories, I do not fully understand what Albert is talking about. But I do know that Sabine and I share the profound distance of being members of two different species. If Sabine needed a last name, it would be Schrödinger.

I always marvel that Sabine appeared at the precise moment when her appearance could not have been spookier.

***

The bottlenose dolphin mothers of the "Enchanted River" mourn when their baby dies. Could not some teens also feel sadness at the loss of the constant company of their mother when left to swim naked among sharks without her?

I have seen many cases of animal behavior on land that we would call mourning if we saw the same behavior in humans. They include mothers with dead babies and adult animals that lost long-time friends. Mourning animals become sluggish and antisocial. Their mourning symptoms may be brief or long-term.

***

It was ironic. I only knew Sabine's Mom because I wanted to see what happens to dolphins who are exposed to coastal construction. The last day we saw Sabine's Mom was the first day of bridge construction over The Pass.

*****

**** A Teaser of Bull Behavior ****

21. As a Matter of Fact, I Will Share

PHOTO BY ANN WEAVER, Ph.D., NOAA 16299, 11/4/2012

Drake Surfaces with a Prize Catch

***

On land, humans do food. The best parties end up in the kitchen as an ancient throwback to when good times literally meant gathering around the campfire to share whatever sizzled among the embers.

Courting couples enjoy countless dinner dates. Party hostesses plan the menu with care. The invitation, "Let's get something to eat," fans the flickers of growing friendship. Restaurants abound. Holiday meals are sacred, like turkey on the American Thanksgiving holiday. Grocery stores battle each other for our food dollars, and then we share the food we buy with family and friends.

Sharing food is basic human behavior. That makes it easy to overlook how unique we are because of it.

People who have two dogs know that they must separate the dogs' food bowls at mealtime because otherwise the dogs could fight. Dogs do not share food. Indeed, most animals do not share food, aggressively so. This is the law of "survival of the fittest." Find your own! Leave mine alone!

Thus, when animals *do* share food, it represents the recognition of the needs of others - which can go both ways.

On a mild autumn day, the hot seas of summer had cooled 10 refreshing degrees. Bottlenose bull Bruce suddenly cruised across *Ms. Behavin's* bow in greeting, surfaced ahead, and returned to his hunt. His bull buddy Drake hunted in the distance. Diana hunted nearby; she and the two bulls had courted all summer. All three dolphins searched in earnest so they were rarely visible. I idled nearby under a cloudy sky.

In the distance off the wake of a passing boat, Drake surfaced with a large Atlantic spadefish in his mouth, which looked like a large, pale angel fish with dark vertical stripes. He started throwing the fish around. I do not think he was playing. Tossing was supposed to accomplish something. Because the fish was too big swallow whole, Drake may have been throwing it around to break it into bite-size pieces. Sometimes he whipped his head sideways, zinging the fish several feet. Sometimes he lay on his back and chucked it a foot or so behind him, but the fish stayed whole.

Then he changed tactics. Floating on his right side, Drake held the fish cross-wise in his mouth and gazed at it until the waters around him calmed too.

This was unprecedented. Galvanized, Bruce and Diana headed over.

Diana swung over to Drake first, chuffed at him, and kept going. Chuffs are cough-like vocalizations used in several contexts. So, it was hard to know what she meant by chuffing at him. But it was expected behavior if Drake was using the survival strategy of "My fish; leave it alone; find your own," and Diana responded with a seaside snarl.

In contrast, Bruce approached his buddy directly. They passed close together but going in the opposite directions. This too was expected behavior if Drake was using the survival strategy of "My fish; find your own," and Bruce kept going without contest.

However, Drake did a somersault, *released his fish* near Bruce, and resumed floating quietly on the water surface. Bruce lifted his head out of the water, rested his chin on Drake's fish, and then took it in his mouth. It was their first hand-off. No scurry or flurry.

PHOTO BY ANN WEAVER, Ph.D., NOAA 1088-1815, 10/17/2007

Bruce "the Beheader" Surfaces with a Faceless Fish

***

When Bruce surfaced again, the fish did not have a face. He lifted the faceless fish out of the water and lay at the surface, mouthing it.

After a time, Drake came back and asked for it: He swam alongside Bruce, slowly, belly to the sky. Pictures show he pressed his left pectoral (arm) fin against Bruce's side, petting him. Then Drake dove backwards with that effortless dolphin command of swimming and vanished underwater.

After a long pause, Bruce followed with the faceless fish.

When they reappeared, Drake had his fish back. This time he floated on his left side, raising the fish in his mouth over the surface. Then Bruce asked for it: He swam alongside Drake, belly to the sky but instead of petting his buddy, he arched strongly. The inverted position is some kind of invitational or begging behavior so his was a greater request.

They submerged. When they reappeared, the fish was gone. Presumably they ate it. No evidence of it floated to the surface.

All this trading took place without one sign of tussle!

***

Back at the lab, I salivated over the pictures that documented this entire event and mulled over the steamy topic of animal food sharing. From what we know, animal food sharing is rare.

Among primates, moms mostly "share" food when they let their clinging infants snack on the crumbs that fall out of their mother's mouth onto their bodies. However, one capuchin monkey I studied at Emory University in Frans de Waal's lab gave her biscuit to her upset infant, which quieted him.[vii] I only saw unquestioned food sharing twice in my years of studying bonobos at the San Diego Zoo: Mother chimp Loretta gave her son Erin a nugget of apple when he was teething and later, when he had all his teeth, a wad of grass she chewed up for him first. However, my gorilla friend Alvila gave me her celery when I gave her M&Ms candies.

Primatologist Frans de Waal showed experimentally that captive capuchins and common chimps have a sense of sharing. For example, capuchins recognize when another monkey is given a better snack than they and are enraged by it. Chimps are more likely to share with other chimps who groomed them earlier that day.

Wild common chimps share food too. Mother chimps who eat nuts after cracking them open with rocks let their infants take nuts from their mouths. Adult males in successful hunting parties share monkey meat but, intriguingly, mainly with females they are currently courting.

The main time when birds and mammals are released from the survival of the fittest "Find your own food" strategy is when they become parents. Under the humbling forces of hormones, animal parents knock themselves out to find Junior enough to eat.

But otherwise, most do not share food, which is why people are asked not to feed animals in the wild or captive settings like zoos. It causes fights.

***

That might not be the only place. Dolphins of the "Enchanted River" share fish in two social settings, one between bonded bull buddies and the other during courtship. So, I might know why Diana chuffed at Drake and then left: He shared his fish with his buddy but NOT with her. So much for bonding during a sizzling summer of courtship!

***

Let us end with that quiet coolness you felt when someone refused the food you offered them.

*****

22. Afterglow

PHOTO BY ANN WEAVER, Ph.D., NOAA 16299, 12/14/2014

Simon and Xavier in Tender Exchange

***

Yes, but can you make love without sex?

As I moved through my academic journey, the premise of the scientific community was to avoid studying animal emotions because it is hard to do well. Unfortunately, that point was lost in translation. Many students came away thinking that animal behavior could be understood by ignoring an animal's emotions, or worse, by assuming that it did not have any emotions. Either way: Stay away from feelings.

Maybe that is why it is more comfortable to think that animals "have sex" or "mate," which many of them do, rather than "make love," which some of them do too. Let's follow the path of affection through the animal kingdom. Backboned animals use all kinds of physical contact to express affection. From people to pigs to parrots, everyone nuzzles affectionately. From monkeys to mice, everyone grooms their partner. Many creatures kiss. People, pygmy chimps, and dolphins go further and have recreational sex – sex with no chance of babies. Recreational sex emerged for dolphins partly because dolphins do not have the anatomical parts to groom each other. Dolphin males also have conscious control over their erections. The necessary sexual equipment is just a thought away. Always handy and very practical.

But making love without sex?

After the cheerful blues of summer, the gray autumn skies seemed particularly muted. Two dolphins appeared in the misty distance. They were about to give us an enchanting glimpse of one of the most wrenchingly tender love scenes I have ever seen.

They were two big bulls. Simon, one of the largest bulls on the "Enchanted River," works alone without a bull buddy, unusual for a bull. Xavier, the second bull, had come to the area two years before this tender exchange and befriended Simon more than had any other bull.

Today they were behaving strangely. It was not strange that they lingered around a sailboat, peering up at the barking bulldog that scampered across the deck on stubby legs. Dolphins and sea dogs have a special relationship because dogs can hear dolphins vocalize and find it quite compelling.

Nor was it strange that a passing yacht temporarily tempted the bulls into action. They vanished into its wake and shot into the skies in a spectacular unison leap, one on each side of the turbulent trail. But surfing was too active. They glided languorously into the shallows behind an island.

They were behaving strangely because they were so *relaxed.* They lulled in absolute languor at the surface, leaning on each other lazily between brief submergences. Each bull in turn floated on his side at the surface, a luxurious but languid invitation. His companion gave an answering nudge or nuzzled up alongside. Gliding just below the surface, they stroked each other with their fins between leisurely breaths of air.

Their luxurious receptivity expanded to us. They approached our boat unhurriedly, even tapping and leaning against its side dreamily. They bathed in its vibrations as they inspected the engine, always out of gear when dolphins are near to avoid maiming them with a spinning propeller.

They reminded me of a couple lounging on a private picnic, toying lightly with themselves and items around them in utter peace. Being dolphins, of course, Simon and Xavier kept swimming. They continued their tender ministrations with drowsy grace into progressively shallower water, where dolphins prefer to socialize.

***

Normally, bottlenose bulls are as "relaxed" as stomping stallions. So their dreamy affection today shot straight into my heart. Coincidentally, I had just finished reading a book by animal behaviorist Marc Bekoff that urged people to see the emotions behind an animal's behavior. Though steeped in scientific training to discount animal emotions, I found today's tenderness impossible to dismiss.

Years before, during a study of captive dolphins, I had watched a dolphin couple make love in this languid, affectionate way. They were male and female so I was not surprised to see them mate. But I was deeply touched by their *tenderness.*

Today, I did not see the bulls mate. In fact, we have never seen *obvious* sex during the many deeply affectionate exchanges like this that we have seen. They may include sex. We just don't see it. What we see is unmistakable tenderness. It takes a hard person not to be struck by it.

***

One part of me felt queasy watching their tenderness, as if it made me a Peeping Tom secretly watching people make love through a window. Another part of me felt undisturbed about watching, because dolphins live in a world without walls where being observed is natural.

Over the millennia, it appears that dolphins have come to understand affection with their companions of either gender as a mechanism for their well-being, beyond mere proliferation of the species. Such affection is an essential language of their survival and not defined by human moral conduct.

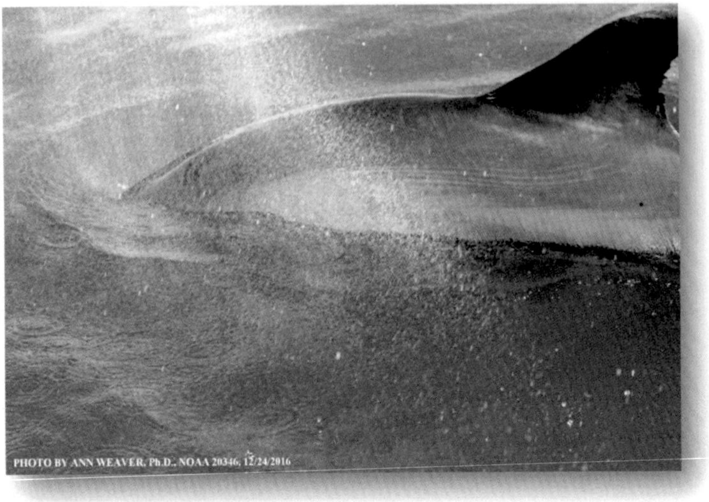

PHOTO BY ANN WEAVER, Ph.D., NOAA 20346, 12/24/2016

Mick Exhales and Makes a Rainbow

***

Dolphin sex at sea remains a deep mystery.

*****

23. Pick on Someone your own Size!

Little Luke goes Flying when Puck Knocks Him out of the Water

***

We have all been somewhere when someone decides to intimidate someone smaller - for whatever reason. When it involves a child, the interaction becomes the highest level of survival. When this happens, we hope for rescue by others better equipped than we. What about at sea?

Three dolphins - mom Lana, her little Luke, and Queen Priscilla's strapping son Puck - were cruising past a tiny islet known as a "junk spoil" created from dredging back into 1950s. Puck, now a junior bull, evidently needed to establish some level of status.

Puck toyed with little Luke as they went. He wove around, over, and under the tiny tyke, prodding him periodically. Puck even carried the tyke on his back now and again by using the same scooping-up maneuver that a mom dolphin uses to protect or transport her tiny newborn: rising underneath it and carrying it briefly on her back. Carrying the tiny tyke on his back, Puck held him "hostage" until little Luke wiggled off.

Superficially, it looked like play. But play is relaxed and fluid. These moves were stilted and stiff.

Other elements were wrong as well. Mainly, little Luke was only four months old and barely out of infancy. Mother dolphins typically only allow infants this age to play very briefly *and* only with very select playmates, which are never young bulls. The exception is when the young bull is the newborn's big brother, but Puck was not Luke's big brother.

Like all dolphins, Puck plays nicely with young calves when he wants. Maybe Lana tentatively trusted him to toy with her tiny tyke because she was friends with his mother. Maybe Puck toyed with her tiny tyke because he dominated her too. In other words, maybe the tiny tyke was not the only dolphin that the junior bull was holding hostage.

Mother dolphins interfere and break up activities involving their calves that do not meet their approval. Yet Lana did not interfere today. Instead, she hovered next to her tiny tyke and the junior bull who jostled him. Hovering suggested she may have been trying to retrieve her baby by siphoning him back into her jet stream. Dolphins can use the envelope of water that surrounds their body to draw a small dolphin to their side. The problem was that Puck could siphon the tiny tyke to his side the same way. Hovering also suggested that Lana was deeply suspicious of all this.

She had good reason to be. Puck soon became rough. The tiny tyke began flopping like a rag doll, a sure sign of trouble. Lana and the young bull started breathing heavily enough to make whale-like cones of visible vapor.

***

That is when a *wall* of dolphins galloped over from the east, almost as if a triumphant musical blast rang out, "Help is here!" The seas became a frenzied mass of gray bodies.

Junior bull Puck may or may not have out-ranked the mother dolphin socially. But he was wholly out-ranked by the four senior bulls who charged up – members of the "Bowery Boys" super-alliance Bruce, Drake, Reggie, and Trevor - like four massive football players rushing to the rescue of someone they have known for years!

Four-against-one was no matter to young Puck, apparently intent on establishing some level of social rank even if he worked alone. He continued playing the maritime counterpart of a 15-year-old punk pushing down a toddler.

In a matter of seconds, a sudden line of froth just under the water surface showed where the tyke rocketed away in a frantic escape from the torpedo rocketing after him. Besieged, the tyke leapt all of the way out of the water. Puck the punk did a flying tackle, and the tyke smacked the water hard.

A frightening new fountain of froth said that Puck had thrown an underwater punch at the calf. Then, with a determined thrust, he lunged out of the water again and knocked the tyke sideways with a direct hit, rolling the tiny tyke into a terrible tumble!

The football players sprinted over again, and all we saw was nothing but swaying water and splashes.

Finally, the waters calmed. Tiny tyke Luke surfaced safely with his mom Lana. Reggie and Trevor flanked them, creating a protective wall.

Puck swam parallel to them some distance away. Infuriated and impotent, he found a horsetail handy for venting his anger - the way a person breaks a pencil instead of punching an irritating coworker. Large ascending bubbles said that heated discussion continued underwater.

Once more Puck tried to approach Lana's winded calf. This time, Bruce and Drake enlarged the protective shield around the mom and her tiny tyke, covering their rear by swimming so close that their faces were awash in the waves from the relieved mom's pumping peduncle.

"The bulls protected that calf!" I cried with relief, but also in disbelief. In the telling, it seems obvious that the four bulls rushed to the rescue of the tiny tyke. But as it was happening, I winced at recollections of scenes like this in other species that turned grisly because incoming individuals created a mindless mob that joined the attack on a victim, with correspondingly serious or deadly injuries – the animal kingdom is no Garden of Eden. Across species, mobbing is more likely than rescue. Unlike mobbing, rescuing is complex mental and physical behavior.

Lana, Luke, and their protective shield headed west. Winded, the tiny tyke clambered onto his mom's back, accomplishing for himself the same scooping-up maneuver that mom dolphins use to protect or transport tiny newborns and which Puck the punk had used against him this very day. It is rare for calves to climb onto their mother's back like this. As a rule, only weakened calves do it.

Dolphin-like, the further they moved from their aggressor, the more they calmed down. After a while, Luke was awash in the stunning sensations of his mother and his heroes finding fish.

Puck the punk did not sprint away for safety, which is what others of his lower social rank have done in these situations. "I'll be back," he seemed to say, as he vented more big belligerent bubbles in vexation but fell further and further behind the departing dolphins.

***

This form of self-expression made the book for several reasons. It is about a bull knocking around a calf while its mother watched helplessly; both behaviors are rare on the "Enchanted River." This combination suggests that dolphins may try to intimate each other indirectly by aiming aggression at an easy victim.

Moreover, this striking episode produced another form of self-expression: a rescue. But what a rescue!

This is the only time we have seen a “wall” of dolphins rush over from a great distance and shatter bad behaviour at sea. Dolphin rescuers tend to work alone when they intervene for another dolphin, as in this book’s story #5 of Clara the Kidnapper and Simon the Savior. Regardless of solo or team efforts, active interventions like these suggest how dolphins might express a sense of justice or fairness.

We have only seen ten episodes of males treating calves roughly in 13 years, with the caveat that there is a misty middle ground that looks rough to us but not to the dolphin mother. Four of the ten episodes involved one to three junior bulls “playing roughly” with a calf whose mother raced nearby, apparently impotent to retrieve it. In all of these, other nearby dolphins intervened on behalf of the harassed. These interventions suggested that intervening dolphins recognized a violation of fair play and acted upon it. The other six episodes involved senior bulls harassing mothers by launching flying tackles at their newborns. In those cases, none of the nearby dolphins intervened.

Intervening dolphins include senior bulls, teen females, and mothers with young calves themselves. In contrast, Luke and Lana’s four fine football player rescuers were clearly coordinated and unquestionably cooperated to rescue Lana and her tiny tyke this day.

***

This was a rare moment when a mother dolphin could not control what happens to her calf. It did not make sense that Lana did not intervene directly. This was not only because of Luke’s tender age but also because Lana has resolutely intervened for calves on other occasions.

***

It is risky to assume that a dolphin has only one way of reacting to a given social situation. For example, the same bull can play gently with one calf but treat another calf roughly. In both cases, the way a bull treats a baby may be a way of reminding its mother of her social rank relative to him. Variability of response is not only a sign of social rank but also of flexibility, taking the current circumstances into account. In this respect I think bottlenose dolphins and people are alike.

Fortunately for Lana and her calf, the "Bowery Boys" came to their rescue. Yet questions remain. Was Puck's aggressive behavior and possibly the death of a calf part of an inherent plan in order to secure the mother for mating? Or was it just an example of the typical frustrations of adolescence?

*****

24. Scraped Knees or Sharpening Swords?

Simon's Scraped Fin

***

Human children who play outside skin their knees and elbows, sometimes from circumstances and sometimes from habit. The child can also use a mirror to look at scabs on body parts they could not see without a mirror, like an elbow. Do skinned knees and mirrors on land have a counterpart at sea?

Florida seasons change leisurely, and one has to pay attention to see them. Some aspects of dolphins change leisurely too. Yet, even when observers think they *are* paying attention, some obvious changes are only obvious later.

One balmy afternoon in early autumn, big bull Simon ascended and exhaled heavily as he cleared the water surface, creating his own geyser of water in which he briefly showered. Sabine, the petite female at his side, rose next to him and breathed the silent breath of a new mother. Her tiny shiny newborn squirted up between them.

Simon, Sabine, and her tiny shiny newborn ambled through pea green waters between some mangrove isles dotting the "Enchanted River." Sabine's baby blurted to the surface in the clumsy way of newborn dolphins. But Simon and Sabine surfaced in an even rhythm, giving the newborn a sustained flowing cadence to follow and perhaps a sweet wave of water to ride like a cradle. Simon's dorsal fin was enormous compared to the tiny newborn fin that surfaced in its shadow.

Swimming leisurely with newborns is one of Simon's specialties. That year's warm months revealed another part of his personality, about which he gave many obvious clues. He wore these clues on his massive dorsal fin in the form of a scrape along its leading or front edge, shown in the picture with this story, that revealed light pink flesh and a bit of blubber underneath.

Even with supreme swimming skills, it is not immediately clear how a dolphin could scrape this part of its body as it does. To visualize this better, what would it take for a person to lightly scrape the bridge of their nose but not any other part of their nose or face while swimming in a strait jacket?

How does Simon do this?

Watching Simon visit Sabine and her baby that day, I saw the scrape on the front of his dorsal fin and noted: "Simon's leading edge wound from this spring is taking a long time to heal. Today, the wound is still flesh colored and a bulge of blubber seems pushed out from the bottom of it. It will leave a big dent in his dorsal fin."

This was early autumn. Does it *really* take six months for a little scrape to heal?

The dolphin dorsal fin, like a sail on its back, is used as a sword and a shield. It is therefore a target for toothraking by other dolphins. It is easy to see how a dolphin can grab another dolphin's dorsal fin with its teeth and leave a trail of parallel lines, each line the mark of a sharp tooth raked across soft skin. It is not easy to see how a dolphin could rake the narrow front edge of another dolphin's dorsal fin in one small spot without leaving other telltale marks. Because it is not easy to understand how this happens, I track every front edge scrape and note if the fin is also marked in other ways that suggest an obvious cause of the scrape, whether toothrakes or another source.

Later, back at the lab, I examined previous photos of Simon's scrape and immediately encountered a mystery, actually two mysteries.

My examination of previous photos solved the first mystery with photographic data though its solution was still hard to believe: Simon's dorsal fin was scraped at least four times between April and September, and the scrapes were so similar that they appeared to be one scrape lasting six months.

Scrape 1 appeared in April. Small bulges of blubber marked the spot. It took a month to heal and fade back to gray. It left a subtle dip in his front edge and appeared to be from toothrakes.

Scrape 2 appeared in June, bigger and more jagged than the previous one. It either enlarged across the month or Simon gained yet another scrape. By July it was eye-catching, hollowed out and bulging with a bit of blubber the size of a wad of chewing gum. This scrape was not from toothrakes.

Like an assembly line, Scrape 3 appeared by August. Careful comparisons of project photos showed that Simon now had a new scrape right below the one that had appeared in June. This scrape also soon bulged with blubber, visible for an entire month as it waxed, waned, and then doubled in size. At one point a short thread of blubber snaked out like a little string of gum that then vanished. The scrape was not obviously from toothrakes.

Each scrape healed to a subtle dent of light gray. The line of small dents from his previous wounds grew again in October when Scrape 4 appeared. This new one was just below the previous wound. The fin was freshly toothraked.

The second mystery remains to be solved. What explains Simon's scrapes and the changes they undergo? How and why did he acquire identical, consecutive scrapes on an unlikely part of his body? That goes for another bull too, Nick, since he sports the same scrapes as Simon, just not as often.

I am intrigued by two possibilities. Let's say his fin is scraped when Simon ducks under a dock but fails to clear it, perhaps miscalculating the distance between the water surface and bottom of a dock and succumbing to slices from its resident barnacles and oysters, much like a child accidently bonks his forehead on a low branch. Or, in the second possibility, do Simon and Nick make some of the scrapes by clipping the dock with their fin intentionally, the way bull moose and elk rub their magnificent antlers on trees to measure how big they are?

*****

**** Category of Its Own ****

25. Who is Innocent among Us?

Vidalia Snaps Playfully at his Mom Valiant

***

The internet is full of dramatic rescues at sea when divers cut entangled dolphins, whales, and whale sharks free of fishing nets and lines. Many entangled animals ask divers to help them or say thank you afterwards, behaviours that require our most profound consideration. How do animals act after the rescue is over and the pain has passed?

The most unique self-expression bestowed upon us thus far came from the shyest mother on the "Enchanted River." We called her Valiant after our shocking introduction as she writhed in pain from a fresh shark bite. She went on to survive and prosper without medical care. Another of her amazing stories centered on an appalling, all-too-frequent event at sea: a dolphin entangled in discarded fishing lines or nets.

One mid-summer day, we found Valiant and her son Vidalia off the pretty little mangrove isle where Valiant often swam. But they did not swim normally. They sprinted around wildly – like they were on fire! It took many minutes to even remotely approach them.

Vidalia Entangled in Fishing Line

***

I should have known. Injured dolphins are very difficult to approach. Valiant's baby boy Vidalia had become entangled in discarded fishing line – monofilament fishing line so strong that it can amputate the fingers of anyone who tries to pull and snap it apart. Fishing line encircled the baby dolphin's little body the way we encircle a wrapped gift with thin bright ribbon pulled terribly tight.

With no thanks to someone who discarded fishing line into the sea like it was a garbage can, the innocent baby dolphin either had been sentenced to a slow death or had to be rescued. We put the first calls into the local stranding network and returned to keep watch at sea.

***

Frustratingly, mom Valiant and tiny Vidalia left the study area and did not return for three months. When we found them again in autumn, Vidalia was still entangled!

Vidalia Leaps Pointlessly to Free Himself from his Noose of Fishing Line

***

Vidalia was jumping and zinging around. To the unpracticed eye, he appeared to be playing. But his jumps and zings were NOT play. They were deadly serious efforts to remove his painful body noose of fishing line, like PeeWee trying to remove her maddening remora.

Have you ever suffered from sand in your eyes, an invisible cactus spine, or the irritating tickle of an undetectable strand of hair? Such tickling begins innocently. When it becomes unrelenting, such "tickling" escalates to taunting and finally to pure torment.

Torment was little Vidalia's life. Fishing line stretched tautly across his mouth like a bridle on a horse, looped around his right pectoral (arm) fin, wrapped up across his back, and cut deep into his dorsal fin. Several more meters of fishing line trailed behind his body, which could have easily tangled with underwater debris like floating palm fronds or crab trap lines, drowning him slowly and horribly.

Every Movement Sliced Vidalia's Skin

***

Every pump of his tail pushed him forward in the water but pulled the fishing line back like a saw cutting wood. Torturously, each movement sliced deeper into his dorsal fin, slit the corner of his mouth more, and rubbed back and forth across his left eye. When Valiant and Vidalia returned to the study area that autumn, this had been going on day and night for at least three months.

To estimate the minimum of this torture, let's say a calf surfaces to breathe twice a minute. At a minimum, Vidalia endured over a quarter million of these saw cuts (350,400) in the four months between the time we first saw him entangled in July and his rescue in November.

Vidalia struggled against his unyielding noose, but to no avail, until he was too weak to struggle any more. Too weary to swim, he repeatedly tried to ride on his mother's back for support. Such behavior is typical of baby hippos, monkeys, and apes, but certainly not of baby dolphins. And baby he was: still young enough to be living solely on his mother's milk.

Seaside Needle in a Haystack

It was possible to catch Vidalia, cut off the fishing line, and release him. But dolphin rescues at sea are equivalent to finding a needle in a seaside haystack. A successful rescue requires that several essential pieces come together at the same time.

Piece one is Federal permission. Fortunately, we had that.

Piece two is the right support. Fortunately, we also had them. These are stranding biologists who are *experienced* in the dangerous mission of netting an entangled dolphin, cutting off the fishing line, doing the world's fastest medical exam, and setting the dolphin free. It takes three dozen of them in multiple boats. Unfortunately, they were scattered across the state of Florida. In other words, *the rescue had to be planned ahead of time rather than launched spontaneously* when we found Vidalia at sea.

Consequently, piece three was to schedule the rescue and then locate Valiant and Vidalia at the scheduled time. Valiant was not equipped with a satellite tag. The only way to know her location was to go out in the boat and find her. Never had the fluid freedom of "free-ranging" dolphins been so overwhelming! We mapped Valiant's sighting locations from the last several years to visualize where she was most likely to be found at sea and searched for her and Vidalia as often as possible.

Piece four was calm weather. Windy days make it impossible to perform the rescue, putting the rescue team and the dolphins at great risk.

Piece five was shallow water. Maritime rescues are dangerous. Dolphins are much bigger and stronger than one would think. Rescues are easiest in hip deep water. Rescuers also hope that the net that is set around the injured dolphin as a temporary infirmary pen does not also accidently include a shark!

***

For countless days, some but not all of the pieces came together. I, along with the other rescuers, chafed with indescribable frustration. However, ours was nothing like the torment of Vidalia's body noose of fishing line slicing him with every move.

Vidalia Strains to be Free as his Mother Appears Helpless to Help

***

Vidalia's Happy Ending

Then, on a November day, after 20 weeks of Vidalia's torment, all the pieces came miraculously together in a sheltered cove.

After much scheduling, the rescue team was finally on its way with an unexpected assembly of 38 people - marine mammal veterinarians, aquarium curators, pathologists, animal handlers, animal trainers, researchers, boat captains, animal behaviorists, and a captain who had the amazing skill of setting a large fishing net around dolphins without mishap.[viii]

Captain John and I set out into the fog at dawn to find the tortured baby and his shy mother. We had done that repeatedly in the days before the rescue. But today, with a large assembly of people and their boats heading our way from all across Florida, we *had* to find Valiant and Vidalia.

In a mystical moment I cannot explain, we found them almost immediately. They swam slowly around the small island near the ramp where the rescuers planned to launch their boats. The dolphins' location could not have been better for the rescue than if they set the net and dove into it themselves.

Next, we had to stay with the dolphins *a stomach-churning two and a half hours* until the rescuers drove across the state, arrived at the boat ramp, completed a half-hour debriefing, launched their boats, and ultimately paraded over.

A boat that is "on dolphins" is only "on dolphins" when dolphins allow it. If dolphins are near a boat, it is because they wish to be. No one can force this to happen, only wish for it very hard.

However, dolphins also wish to be around boats handled with the splendid flow of boat captains who know how to drive around them, which is a hard-won art form. Granted, the dolphins' cooperation was essential that morning. But Captain John's silky management of our research boat in those trying hours of staying near, but not too near or too far, was a textbook example of the day.

A Mystifying Manipulation

In the hours before the rescue, Valiant and Vidalia had been calm. Valiant swam near the boat, though she periodically shot forward to snatch a breakfast fish. Vidalia had been uncharacteristically sedate too. He did not throw himself about in frantic attempts to rid himself of his taunting body noose as he had done every other day that autumn. Other than the stomach-churning tension on board as we tried to stay with them until the flotilla of rescue boats arrived, the scene was the kind that dolphin behaviorists cherish.

Finally debriefed and launched, the flotilla of eight rescue boats approached like a slow parade going past. As they did, Valiant switched from drowsy to wide awake. She swam towards the parade of rescue boats, dove for a moment, and then like a medieval king riding towards the enemy's lines with his colors raised, suddenly shot half way out of the water holding a big, bright yellow coil in her mouth - a fresh whelk egg case!

Valiant Prepares to Launch the Bright Yellow Whelk Egg Case

***

With a mighty sideways snap, she whipped the bright yellow egg case several feet to the right. It hit the water and vanished along with Valiant. Rescuers yelped, *"What was that?!"* I wondered, "*Why* was that?"

Snapping the bright yellow egg case made Valiant instantly obvious to everyone. Unless that was her point, her gesture seemed dramatically out of context. This was no time to play - of course, the rescuers knew that. Why should Valiant? Moreover, she had shown no inclination to play earlier that morning.

Did she snap the bright yellow egg case because she was scared? Valiant was completely free to retreat from the boats, which dolphins do with great facility whenever so inclined.

Whipping the bright yellow whelk egg case into the air seemed dramatically out of place. And it was hard to say why she did it.

Maybe she did it in justifiable frustration because those dull-witted humans still failed to understand that the dolphins had made themselves available and it was time to get on with the rescue.

Valiant and Vidalia allowed us to remain near them until the net was set around them, the rescuers were on the water, and the vets carefully tended the baby dolphin. During the rescue, the mom dolphin maintained her steady whistling vigil with no sign of aggression towards the rescuers.

***

PHOTO BY RANDY WELLS UNDER MMPA/ESA PERMIT NO. 932-1489-09, 11/15/2011

Nine-month-old Vidalia during his Rescue
He looks calm in this picture, but I reached out and laid my hand on him briefly. His heart was beating wildly.

***

Several minutes later the net opened like a yawn, and the two dolphins raced back to each other and out of the net.

Everyone exploded into excited jubilation because the rescue had gone perfectly. We were all so relieved. Captain John and I wanted to stay and celebrate the resounding success of the rescue with the others, but we had to leave. It was important to watch Vidalia for signs of shock, although we certainly did not want to harass the dolphins further. Understandably rattled by the rescue, would Vidalia show generally normal behavior until he swam to the other side of an island and died of a heart attack?

We excused ourselves from the celebrating rescuers and trailed the dolphins very cautiously. Unexpectedly, they waited for us. They allowed us to trail them at a diplomatic distance, which we did for a short time.[ix] I was astonished that the mother dolphin Valiant let us draw near like that. How was she supposed to know we only meant well for her son?

***

Vidalia rescue team leader, Dr. Randall Wells of the Chicago Zoological Society, was also impressed by the fact that Valiant and Vidalia stayed so close to the net after their release, hung around for many minutes, and only then slowly swam away. More typically, based on his experiences over the past 40 years with occasional capture and release of dolphins for rescues and health assessments, dolphins released from temporary captures will flee the capture site at great speed although they are often seen swimming calmly some distance away within minutes.

Later that day, Captain Jack Steeves and First Mate Lani Grano of a local dolphin tour boat called to say they were watching Vidalia jumping and leaping. This time, they felt sure, he was jumping for joy.

***

Vidalia's rescue at sea involved netting him along with his mother and then holding them together in the temporary pen. That meant that the mother dolphin was in the pen with the vet team as they held her calf and cut off the fishing line.

In contrast, during other animal captures in the course of my animal behavior work, a baby animal that needed veterinary care was separated from its mother so she did not attack the vet staff in protecting her baby.

Knowing the protective zeal of these other animal mothers whose babies were being tended, before the rescue I asked the federal stranding team coordinator Blair Mase Guthrie what to expect of the mother dolphin's behavior during the rescue. She said, "You know, Ann, it is **so** weird. They seem to," she paused and then continued slowly, "u_n_d_e_r_s_t_a_n_d that we are helping them."

This is a profound mystery of dolphin social psychology.

Not Too Rattled by the Rescue

We did not find Valiant and Vidalia for a month after the rescue. Had we lost their trust? When we did find them, it was in a hidden cove off of the "Enchanted River." They had not vanished the moment they heard us coming. That was encouraging.

Valiant hunted with a particular gait that carved a trail of smooth circular footprints across lightly ruffled blue-green waters. Consequently, we tracked her easily. She continued with her hunt despite our presence, which was another good sign.

Vidalia stayed near his mom while she hunted. He momentarily displayed the right side of his tailstock, still chafed a month after the relentless slapping of fishing line. The yawning dent at the base of his dorsal fin, created by five uncompromising months of fishing line sawing it off his body, had begun to heal.

After some minutes, they converged and headed out side by side. Valiant moved them ever closer to the boat, glancing at us across the water surface and then slowly gliding under the bow.

What was most eloquent about our first encounter with Valiant and Vidalia after the rescue was its lack of drama. The dolphins had behaved naturally and remained relaxed throughout. We had not lost their trust.

Humbling Sense of Gratitude

Despite his horrific beginning, Vidalia developed normally. His big move to independence from his shy mother Valiant finally came in early 2015.

For the next two years, Vidalia alternated between feeding and solitude. Mostly, as per the adolescent "Phantom Phase," we would glimpse him and then he would be gone. This was normal.

Yet, what makes studying dolphins so fascinating is the spin they put on "normal." One spring day in 2017, Vidalia was alone but allowed us near. He even surfaced alongside the boat for a couple of companionable surfaces, and then headed to a field of mud plumes rising like somber tan thunderheads in pea green waters. We followed and put the boat in neutral. Waiting for his next surface, I squinted in disbelief. One of the mud plumes was moving with slow motion ripples across the surface. Vidalia had led us to a trio of mud pluming manatees, and then vanished!

A Manatee Peers up from the Water Surface

***

Vidalia's companionable surfaces reminded me of his shy mom Valiant. Every time we approached her after we rescued her baby boy in November 2011, Valiant would stop whatever she was doing, come over, and swim companionably alongside our boat for several minutes, as Vidalia had done today. Most dolphins behave this way on occasion. Only Valiant, the mother of the baby dolphin we rescued, came over and swam alongside us *every time she saw us* during the four years that followed the rescue. She was thanking us.

Thus, some of the most gracious behavior I have ever been offered in my life came from a wild dolphin. We never touched, yet touched each other deeply. There is nothing more humbling than the gratitude of a wild dolphin. The most notable of Valiant's many amazing behaviors was her *obvious gratitude.*

Thus, it is with considerable regret that I report that Valiant said "Thank You" again on what turned out to be the last day we saw her.

Valiant Glancing at the Boat

***

It was a February day, the "Enchanted River" a soft but somber palette of grays. Valiant was there with Vidalia and attentive bulls Nick and Rick. She slid through the jade-colored waters over to the boat with her usual "Thank You." That was the last day we ever saw her.

Intellectually, I knew I had been watching Valiant age. I was emotionally unprepared to realize I had been watching her age, sicken, and die.

Now I see what a privilege it is to take the whole ride of life, going to the very end to make that circle complete.

***

Valiant lived a long life. Not everyone on the "Enchanted River" does.

Like Vidalia. He died when he was only six years old. The necropsy revealed that he had been stabbed twice with sting ray barbs, one in his heart and another in his lung. It took him six weeks to die.

*****

Bon Voyage

The never-ending ebb and flow of life continues, but our time with the secrets behind the dolphin smile stops here. The 25 amazing things dolphins do along the "Enchanted River" reveal a complex society organized to face challenges that, in many ways, parallel the challenges we face in our own human society.

This dolphin society has rules of conduct. Dolphins protect each other; respond to injury and death, sometimes severely; and suffer the consequences of failing to follow the rules.

Members of this society depend on each other and have a corresponding flair for showmanship. All ages draw on an impressive array of creative tactics for attracting the attention of other dolphins, vital for navigating large social networks and affectionate relationships that can last for decades while avoiding danger.

Through behavior towards the boat, the dolphins exhibit an unusual interest in another society: humanity. Their interest involves occasional reversals of who studies whom, apparently triggered by changes in human routines, and tests to see what a dolphin can make a boat do. The dolphins' interest in us also involves attempts to communicate; potential teasing; inadvertent episodes that keep observers alert; and sometimes, very strange timing indeed.

The bull bottlenose dolphins of the "Enchanted River" have, imbedded within the larger society, a second smaller society with its own rules, ranks, and ramifications. It is based on bonding strongly, sharing food, exchanging affection, protecting others, and perhaps examining the self.

As in human society, members of the dolphin society must remain aware of and avoid dangers, but cannot avoid the ones about which they are naïve. Fishing line entanglement is an unforgivable crime on the high seas, and the final secret behind the dolphin smile revealed an astonishing capacity for gratitude.

It's Up to Us!

Don't let the ebb and flow of life on the "Enchanted River" stop here.

I hope these glimpses of life at sea show the similarity of not only dolphins, but animals of many types, to ourselves. Our joint responsibility is to keep an open mind to all species and share the task of assuring our mutual habitats and survival.

Their gifts may be subtle. But they ensure our ability to learn from them on a broader scale than on our daily grind. Perhaps we can even make our own societies better if we pay attention.

May you find your own "Enchanted River." It may be in the mountains, the forests, the shore, or the deserts. It could be in city parks, in your backyard, even out your window.

Join me in marveling.

PHOTO BY ANN WEAVER, Ph.D., NOAA 16299, 5/19/2012

Are You a Finatic Yet?

[i] **Ann Weaver's Species Life List (Animals I have worked with directly or studied)**
PRIMATES: Allen's Swamp Monkeys, Bonnet Macaques, Bonobos, Capuchins, Celebes Crested Macaques, Cotton Top Tamarins, Douc Langurs, Drills, Goeldi's Monkeys, Gorillas, Hamlyn's Guenons, Kikuyu Colobus, L'Hoests Guenons, Mantled Howlers, Orang-utans, Pigtailed Macaques, Pygmy Marmosets, Red Howlers, Mandrills, Ring-tailed Lemurs, Squirrel Monkeys, Spider Monkeys, Talapoins, Woolly Monkeys
MARINE MAMMALS AND SEA CREATURES: Bottlenose Dolphins, Spotted Dolphins, Striped Dolphins, Common Dolphins, Pacific White-sided Dolphins, Elephant Seals, Sea Lions, Whale Sharks, Giant Manta Rays, Sperm Whales, Fin Whales, Blue Whales, Bryde's Whales, Pilot Whales, Risso's Dolphins, Manatees
CARNIVORES: Alaskan Brown Bears, Black-footed Cat, Canadian Wolf, Cape Hunting Dogs, Cheetahs, Chinese Wolves, Corsack Foxes, Cougars, Fennec Foxes, Fishing Cat, Grisons, Hyenas, Large-spotted Genet, Manchurian Brown Bears, Margay, Polar Bears, Red Pandas, Short-clawed Otters, Siberian Tigers, Sloth Bear, Small-spotted Genet, Spectacled Bears, Spot-necked Otters, Sumatran Tiger, Sun Bears, Zorillas
SMALL MAMMALS: Anteaters, Binturong, Dwarf Mongoose, Echidna, European Red Squirrels, Hedgehogs, Hutia, Hyrax, Kinkajous, Meerkats, Patagonian Cavies, Prevost's Squirrels, Tree Shrews
UNGULATES: Addra Gazelle, Altai Wapiti, Anoas, Axis Deer, Babirusa, Bactrian Wapiti, Baird's Tapirs, Barbados Sheep, Bawean or Kuhl's Deer, Bharals or Blue Sheep, Blackbuck, Chinese Water Deer, Cretan Goats, Cuvier's Gazelle, Dybowski's Sika, European Wild Boar, Formosan Sika Deer, Greater Kudu, Guanaco, Lesser Kudu, Manchurian Sika Deer, Mhorr Gazelle, Mouflon Sheep, Nilgiri Tahr, Nubian Ibex, Pampas Deer, Pot-bellied Pigs, Pronghorn Antelope, Pygmy Hippo, Red River Hogs, Roan Antelope, Roe Deer, Slender-horned Gazelles, Somali Wild Asses, Takins, White-bearded Gnu, White-lipped Deer, White-tailed Deer, Wood Bison
MARSUPIALS: Flying Squirrels, Goodfellows Tree Kangaroos, Koalas, Ring-tailed Possum, Tree Kangaroo, Virginia Opossum
BIRDS: Abyssinian Hornbills, Amazon Parrots, Barn Owl, Blue Jays, Brown Pelicans, Burrowing Owl, Caracara, Cockatiels, Cockatoos, Conures, Cormorants, Crows, Doves, Emus, Finches, Grackles, Great Blue Herons, Great Horned Owl, Guam Rails, Kestrel, Lesser Egrets, Lories, Lorikeets, Lovebirds, Macaws, Milky Storks, Mockingbirds, Moor Hens, Nighthawks, Night Herons, Ostrich, Pelicans, Pigeons, Pileated Woodpeckers, Quail, Red Knots, Red-shouldered Hawk, Red-tailed Hawk, Screech Owls, Spectacled Owl, Thrushes, Toucans, Trumpeter Swans, Warblers, Waterfowl, White Storks
REPTILES:Ball Pythons, Boa Constrictors, Dumeral's Boas, Corn Snakes, Cunningham's Skinks, Dwarf Chameleons, Florida Alligators, Garter Snakes, Gould's Monitor Lizards, Green Iguana, Hermit Crabs, Indigo Snakes, Jackson's Chameleons, King Snakes, Nile River Monitor Lizard, Rat Snakes, Rosy Boas, Taiwanese Beauty Snakes, Terrapins, Veiled Chameleons
FISH: Experience with freshwater and saltwater aquaria
DOMESTICS: Chinchillas, Domestic Goats (Saanens, Pygmies, Alpine, Toggenburgs, Nubians, LaManchas, etc.); Domestic Pigeons (Helmets, Tumblers, Chinese Owls, Etc.); Domestic Sheep (Shropshires, Karakuls, Colombians, Cheviots, Suffolks, Hampshires, Jacobs, Southdowns, etc.); Dexter Cows, Ferrets, French Lop Rabbits, Guinea Pigs, Llama, Horses, Malamutes, Miniature Horses, Mules, Neapolitan Mastiffs, St. Bernards, Tibetan Mastiffs

[ii] There are three general scenarios that involve a playing calf and its mother that, as with humans, depends on the age of the youngster. The scenario when Bette "rescued" calf Celine was that of an older calf playing while its mom went about her business in the general area. Mom was presumably monitoring the playmates. She is presumably content with the situation *because* she stays in the general area without drawing near. If she is not content with her calf's situation, she will intervene.

[iii] Weaver, A., & Kuczaj, S. (2016). Neither toy nor tool: Grass-wearing behavior among free-ranging bottlenose dolphins in Western Florida. International Journal of Comparative Psychology, 29, uclapsych_ijcp_31885. Retrieved from http://scholarship.org/uc/item/893417x3

[iv] Dolphin Watch newspaper column http://www.tbnweekly.com/editorial/outdoors/

[v] A&E TV Special on animal emotions 2000. 2010. Interview with Ann Weaver, Ric O'Barry, and Lori Marino on Animal Suicide, by Vicky Collins, Huffington Post: http://www.huffingtonpost.com/vicky-collins/can-dolphins-commit-suici_b_592856.html

[vi] Habituation is far more than simply familiarizing the animals with us and with the process of being observed. As in any developing relationship, there is increasing habituation over time. It takes way more time to accomplish than I ever expected.

Habituation is a process with many layers. One layer of habituation is acclimating animals to human presence. Zoo animals, of course, do not have a choice about being on display all day; however, many zoos recognize this and have done what they can to give their animals a private place away from people. Another layer is acclimating animals to long periods of close observation. A third layer is the point where an animal is no longer inhibited by observation, that is, when they stop *changing the details of their lives* and act the way nature designed them to act (without alterations because observation still inhibits them).

The result of increasing habituation is that we continue to see new dolphin behaviors. I naturally wonder whether I am improving my observational eye for quick dolphin behavior, and that has to be true to some extent. But it seems more likely to me that the dolphins are in fact showing us more of the intricacies of their behavior as they become more used to us and trust us more.

Instead of seeing everything the first year or two, we see more and more details all the time. One of many examples: Short-term studies often report that all of the dolphins in a group do the same thing (everyone is traveling, everyone is feeding, etc.). In contrast, local dolphins often do just the opposite: Everyone is "doing their own thing." Such differences may be related to the level of habituation to the research boat. Dolphins unused to being followed and observed may feel threatened, draw together protectively, and behave uniformly like a school of fish out of caution until the threat goes away. In contrast, consider an instance in November 2014 when we were allowed to watch a tender courtship exchange between bull Rick and female Bette at close range. Bette nuzzled up against Rick and then moved a short distance away with her tongue hanging out! Remember, this happened under the water at sea with us watching from a small boat. The *only* reason we saw it was because Bette and Rick let us see it. However, it did take an investment of 10 years of study to see. It also took 10 years for the dolphins to reveal that they will make a mud plume, then turn around and swim through it when they are not using it to trap fish to eat. Whether the mud plume is yet another form of object handling in the context of courtship, some kind of self-maintenance behavior, or something else altogether remains to be seen.

This pristine state of acceptance, such as Bette and Rick letting us watch their courtship, is hard won because it requires trust. Trust is expensive in both money and time. Trust and habituation go hand in hand. Habituation is critical to accuracy. True understanding of another species requires years of relationship building so that the presence of observers does not eliminate those rare but significant behaviors from observation.

Until trust is accomplished, we presumably only glimpse rare behaviors (such as whelk wearing, food sharing, protecting the wounded, and mourning the dead) and then assume they are rare. Some of them probably are rare. But like a broken heart, occurring rarely does not reduce their significance. All of them help us understand a species better.

Bottom line: The dolphins we study are becoming less inhibited around us all the time because of the time we invest in this effort. This is a vital consideration, especially when working with members of a highly intelligent species. The more animals of a given species *watch each other* and the more self-aware they are, the harder it is to acclimate them to the close observation needed to understand them. In fact, I bet that the ease of habituation is strongly and inversely related to the species' level of self-awareness.

The discovery of ever-more information about dolphin behavior is like a rose opening with fresh new petals forever. This argues that bottlenose dolphins ARE self-aware *because* they can be inhibited by the presence of strangers. They are far more difficult to habituate than I ever expected.

[vii] www.emory.edu/LIVING_LINKS

[viii] The rescue team was a massive assembly of 38 people, from Argosy University Sarasota, Sea World Orlando, University of Florida Gainesville, Tampa Bay Aquarium, Clearwater Marine Aquarium, Marine Mammal Pathobiology Lab, Florida Wildlife Commission, National Marine Fisheries Service, National Oceanic and Atmospheric Administration, and Mote Marine Aquarium. We are particularly indebted to Blair Mase Guthrie of NOAA and Dr. Randall Wells of the Chicago Zoological Society: Without their support, this never would have happened.

[ix] Captain John Heidemann and myself, Clearwater Marine Aquarium's Abby Stone and Skip Jackson, and The Florida Aquarium's Kristen Aanerud.

29759223R00088

Made in the USA
San Bernardino, CA
17 March 2019